PRAISE FOR

THE LIFER

Reading Russ' stories from the golden era of rock climbing is incredibly inspiring, featuring snapshots of some of the most relevant climbers and areas and routes of our sport. Not only is it a great personal account of finding one's way in the world of climbing but also brings to life some of the incredible characters, climbing areas, and routes that ushered in modern day climbing.

—Chris Sharma

The Lifer is a riveting tale for those who climb and those who don't. Russ takes us up the world's most harrowing ascents, introducing us to the pantheon of rock-climbing greats along the way, but his most compelling journey is the one he takes within, building faith in himself, one move at a time, dangling high above where most mortals fear to tread.

—Arthur O. Sulzberger, Jr.
Chairman Emeritus, The New York Times Company

This book is part climbing history, part memoir, and part travelogue. Russ has personally experienced many of the pivotal moments in modern climbing—this book offers a first-hand account of where climbing came from and how it's changed over his many decades in the sport. There's an old saying that when you start climbing: It's all about what you climb. Then it becomes more about where you climb, and eventually it's about who you climb with. Russ' many decades as a climber travel this same arc, from seeking out the hardest routes to exploring interesting new areas to savoring certain climbing partnerships. I was moved and I laughed out loud.

—Alex Honnold

Having been the first American to travel abroad to many of the most historic climbing areas throughout the world, Russ' colorful and hilarious stories depict the essence of climbing culture as it evolved from the dirtbag days of death defying first ascents, to the development of climbing areas across the globe, to the current status as a mainstream Olympic sport.

—Lynn Hill

What a fabulous journey through the evolution of modern climbing told through the eyes of one of its most dedicated and passionate students! Russ' stories of his climbing escapades all over the world through the decades shed light on how the sport came to be and also offers a personal glimpse into what climbing gives us: lifelong partnerships, an exploration of who we are, and why we choose to live this life of adventure. It is a nostalgic, hilarious, and celebratory story that will leave you inspired to live out your own dreams.

—Emily Harrington

The Lifer illustrates how exciting a climbing life can be. Russ's stories take us rock climbing around the US, to Australia and back; through the evolution of the sport from Germany to South Korea, encompassing adventure climbing ethics with its spicy risks to modern redpoint sport climbing and the pursuit of pure difficulty. It's about making new friendships and cherishing old ones, while taking a trip through climbing history and Russ's own evolution from dirtbag climber to a business man who brought his spirit and love of climbing to help build an iconic brand in the outdoor industry.

—Babsi Zangerl

If you're a climber, you'll love this memoir. Russ Clune has been everywhere, climbed everything, with a tremendous cast of partners and friends, and he has the natural storyteller's ability to keep you with him every step of the way. There is a close-grained history of modern climbing here as well as his own pilgrim's progress. If you're not a climber, welcome to a full-blown obsession. Feel the burn, the fear, the joy, the horror, and learn a new language without risking life and limb.

—William Finnegan
Author of *Barbarian Days: A Surfing Life*

THE LIFER

Rock Climbing Adventures in
The Gunks and Beyond

The Lifer: Rock Climbing Adventures in The Gunks and Beyond
is published under Catharsis, a sectionalized division under
Di Angelo Publications, Inc.

Catharsis is an imprint of Di Angelo Publications.
Copyright 2023.
All rights reserved.
Printed in the United States of America.

Di Angelo Publications
Headquarters: 4265 San Felipe #1100, Houston, Texas 77027
Distribution: 250 Main Ave N, Twin Falls, ID 83301
Subsidiary Rights: 4209 Santa Monica Blvd #200, LA, CA 90029

Library of Congress
The Lifer: Escapades in The Gunks and Beyond
ISBN: 978-1-955690-51-5
Paperback

Words: Russ Clune
Photos (unless otherwise noted): Russ Clune
Cover Photo: Matt Calardo
Cover Design: Savina Deianova
Interior Design: Kimberly James
Editors: Matt Samet, Willy Rowberry

No part of this publication may be reproduced, distributed,
or transmitted in any form or by any means without the prior
written permission of the publisher, except in the case of brief
quotations embodied in critical reviews and certain other
noncommercial uses permitted by copyright law. For permission
requests, contact info@diangelopublications.com.

For educational, business, and bulk orders, contact
distribution@diangelopublications.com.

1. Sports & Recreation --- Rock Climbing
2. Sports & Recreation --- Extreme Sports
3. Biography & Autobiography --- Sports

THE LIFER

Rock Climbing Adventures in
The Gunks and Beyond

RUSS CLUNE

For Mayv.

As Helen Keller said,
"Life is either a daring adventure or nothing."

Make it adventurous.

CONTENTS

FOREWORD

The 1980s—When It All Began

I feel fortunate to have been a child of the 1980s, a pivotal decade during which so much was invented that forms the fabric of our lives today. We had our first truly portable personal stereo— the Sony Walkman. Our first cell phones, like the hilariously giant Motorola DynaTac 8000X Michael Douglas's character, Gordon Gekko, wields on the beach in *Wall Street.* Our first personal home computers—the Apple, the IBM 5150, the Commodore 64. Our first VCRs, which let us enjoy Hollywood movies in our living rooms, just as these movies began using special effects that were actually convincing, as with *Indiana Jones and the Raiders of the Lost Ark* (1981) or *The Terminator* (1984). So much of the technology developed during the Industrial Age was coming to fruition, infusing and helping us reinvent our lives in ways both exciting and novel.

This held true also for rock climbing, the central topic of this book, in a historically rich era retold vibrantly on these pages through the eyes of one of its most talented, dedicated, and fervent practitioners, Russ Clune. Ropes and harnesses had become light and reliable, lead protection had leapt ahead light years with the introduction of the spring-loaded camming device, sticky butyl rubber (*goma cocida*—"cooked rubber"—from Spain) had fostered exponential leaps in difficulty whose ripples are still spreading to this day, and training tools like hangboards, climbing gyms, and home walls had begun to crop up across America. I first began climbing in 1987 when many of these tools were already common, learning in the relative climbing backwater of New Mexico. Still, I followed the news of our sport voraciously, reading every issue of *Climbing, Mountain,* and *Rock & Ice* cover to cover, memorizing the names of the hardest climbs and the superheroes who dared to try them.

Many of those names appear in this book, and one of those names is Russ Clune, the pioneering Shawangunks free climber and author of the first free solo—a ropeless ascent—of the ferocious *Supercrack* (5.12+) at his home area, a feat still unrepeated to this day.

It is hard to underestimate the catalyzing effect that Russ and his peers had on American (and global) rock climbing. Until the 1970s and 1980s, so much of rock climbing had been about getting up the wall using whatever tactics, often direct aid and resting on the rope, or using the protection as handholds to pull past cruxes in the "French free" style. But this new generation of *free climbers,* of which Russ was a key member as a young upstart at the Gunks, realized you could link the rock's natural features without resting, doing the climbs in impeccable style. Then they traveled to Europe and saw "sport climbing," with expansion bolts placed on rappel to protect difficult face climbs. They also saw climbers "hangdogging"—rehearsing the moves after they fell, allowing them to feel the holds and imprint sequences in order to make quick ascents of the hardest climbs, instead of lowering off each time they fell. Combined, these advents advanced rock climbing at a lightning pace that remains unmatched since.

A huge part of the spread of this new style was travel, in a pre-Internet era when ideas could only be disseminated face-to-face or through print. There were also just so few of us interested in climbing hard, and so few areas to test ourselves, that everyone seemed to know everyone—or at least who the major players were—and we'd run into each other at the same crags. I came in at the tail end of all this, as a starry-eyed kid one generation behind Russ, Wolfgang Güllich, Lynn Hill, Todd Skinner, and others, all of whom I looked up to and would eventually meet, if not climb with. But my youth and relative inexperience did not keep me from embracing the changes they'd wrought, and I and so many of my peers soon became proponents of and lifelong devotees to sport climbing, which I still pursue some thirty-six years later.

What is most compelling to me about *The Lifer* is how deftly Russ weaves these many threads together, in a rollicking but also honest and emotional look at that time in his life as a young man, and how he rode and helped propel the evolutionary wave sweeping the sport. If you've ever met Russ, you'll know he's one of the friendliest, funniest, most gregarious guys at the crag, a magnetic personality known as much for his storytelling as his grace on the stone. His unique voice jumps off these pages, as he gives you front-row seats to apocryphal tales from that era—Strappo's Mountain Room Bar antics in Yosemite, Wolf's epic whippers in the Elbsandstein, drama at the Bardonecchia competition—that, as it emerges in the retelling, actually did happen and are maybe even nuttier than you thought!

It's hard not to be nostalgic for the 1980s—for MTV, the neon colors, new wave music, yuppies, movie soundtracks with synth keyboards and saxophones. It's hard also not to be nostalgic for what it meant to be a climber during that decade—the empty crags, virgin rock, free camping everywhere, and a headlong feeling of standing at the precipice of major change. I can think of no better guide to and travelogue partner for that special era than Russ, and I hope you enjoy reading *The Lifer* as much as I have.

—Matt Samet

INTRODUCTION

Rock climbing has come a long way since I took it up in 1977. Few would have called it a sport back then. It was a fringe activity, done on the margins of society, by a somewhat eccentric gang of people. Climbers were predominantly white, male, and young. For some reason, perhaps because of the problem-solving nature of it, rock climbing also attracted nerds. Scientists and mathematicians were common, at least on my home cliffs—the quartz-conglomerate bluffs of the Shawangunks in New York State. Females were few and far between, and those who did brave the scene were strong both physically and emotionally; they had to be to survive the onslaught of sometimes undesired male attention.

Rock climbing in the seventies was still a sub-genre of mountain climbing. Many adherents considered climbing small cliffs nothing more than practice for the great ranges around the world. As a result, climbers followed the same basic principles for a short cliff as they would a Himalayan giant: they started at the bottom with little knowledge of what lay ahead and got to the top using whatever means necessary and as quickly as possible. After all, it was simply practice for the real thing: the big mountains.

But there was change in the air. Rock climbing, for some, had become an end in itself. These dedicated rock climbers had little desire to head to the hills, to suffer cold and wind, to expose themselves to the pain of altitude and the objective dangers of mountain climbing. They just wanted to tackle ever-more-difficult rock climbs. I would turn out to be one of these people.

I grew up in Mamaroneck, a suburb just a short drive north of New York City. Winged Foot Golf Club, where my father regularly played the game, was my backyard, so my childhood was filled with swimming and golf from age five through my adolescent years. While I enjoyed those sports, I eventually became bored of them and was drawn to the outdoors as a young teen. For me, getting outside was an escape. While I liked the actual game of golf, I didn't enjoy the trappings around it, especially the country-club snobbery centered on the type of car a family drove or the size of their house. I found peace in the woods and a place where double-knit trousers and a polo shirt could be replaced by cut-off shorts and a dirty tee.

No one in my family was outdoorsy. My father was a busy lawyer, the man in the gray flannel suit, growing his practice and making money to keep me and my three younger siblings fed. My mother was tasked with corralling our energies and keeping us out of trouble as best she could. To help teach me discipline, my parents decided I'd spend the first eight grades of my education at an all-boys Catholic school, suffering the beatings and humiliations that went with it. I grew to hate school and to question not only the religious teachings but my parents' entire lifestyle. However, nobody bothered me while I explored our nearby woods.

I read every book I could find in our local library about hiking, camping, and, most intriguingly, mountain climbing. Colin Fletcher's *The Complete Walker* helped me figure out how to take hikes and camp in the forest. Weekends out in local state parks were followed by longer and longer hikes along the Appalachian Trail. Maurice Herzog's *Annapurna* lit up dreams of heroic adventure on the high peaks of the planet. Going hiking was one thing, but climbing was another. All I could do was read about climbing. No one in my suburban world climbed mountains—at least, no one I knew. The most experienced person I could muster was an acquaintance who'd earned a merit badge in the Boy Scouts for rappelling. Climbing would have to wait until I went to college.

Today, rock climbing is a sport—and an Olympic one at that. Climbing gyms, something that didn't even exist as a concept when I began climbing, are now everywhere—as of 2022, there were over 600 gyms in the United States and Canada alone. Plus, climbing is all over the media, from podcasts to advertisements to major motion pictures. Odds are, the average parent has probably taken their kids to a birthday party held at a local climbing gym. Rock climbing itself has also changed dramatically, splitting into a variety of subdisciplines.

To be a rock climber when I started meant one thing: you climbed rocks, big and small. We also had one particular set of "rules," which today might fall under the rubric of "traditional" climbing: you began at the bottom, placing your own protection as you went. The rope was only there to catch a fall, not to hang on to rehearse the moves, nor could you rappel in from above to inspect the moves or to install fixed protection like bolts (though you could painstakingly place these with a hand drill from stances, climbing ground-up and doing so only sparingly). For your ascents to be considered credible by your peers, you needed to do things the old-school way, rooted in the traditions of mountain climbing.

Today's climbers can choose to specialize in a particular aspect of rock climbing, or they can mix and match as the fancy strikes them. They may only be into bouldering, testing their power on short climbs over a bed of crashpads without the need of a rope. Maybe it's sport climbing, in which expansion bolts placed on rappel provide the protection. Or they might be traditional climbers—like we all used to be, before the activity splintered into its various flavors—placing their own gear into cracks as they ascend. Today, I know many who will only climb in a gym, with no desire to even bother with real cliffs or who focus solely on competitions on artificial walls. There is even a subset of participants specializing in speed—climbers who race up a fifteen-meter wall in blisteringly fast times. To top it off, there are different rules and cultures for each discipline. If you're exceptionally talented, you can make a living as a professional climber through sponsorships with companies ranging from specialty outdoor brands to automobile manufacturers. This was virtually impossible a few decades ago, no matter how good you were—even the best climbers of the 1980s, when the concept of climbing sponsorship began, were rarely earning a living wage and needed to supplement their incomes with part-time jobs.

What drew me to climbing remains a complex question, and to this day I can't give a fully satisfactory answer, even to myself. It certainly wasn't the money. Surely, part of it was adolescent rebellion, but it was way more than that. I was searching for something beyond the fairways of a golf course and beyond the world of my parents, whose lives, despite how much I loved them, I found to be soul-crushingly dull. I yearned to be outdoors, in big country. Conforming didn't work for me, and I needed adventure.

As soon as I touched rock, climbing became my passion. I felt it on my first climb, in Bolton, Vermont: a mixture of fear, amazement, and exhilaration. My world transformed into a life in which work and a career fell well down the list of priorities, and the big decisions were which cliffs and countries to visit. My life *became* climbing. It wasn't a lifestyle; it was *life*.

The world was a place to explore, with rock climbing as my vocation and sole reason to travel. Information then was scant; there were no climbing guidebooks to anything but the most well-known and popular destinations, so like all climbers of that era, I relied on magazine articles and word-of-mouth to plan my trips. It was a world of letter writing, travelers' cheques, rolling the dice, and hoping intuition paired with a sketchy roadmap would be enough. To the "normal" world and to my parents, my rock climbing and the compromises that went with it—living in the back of my pickup for months at a time, showering infrequently, surviving on cheap ramen noodles—was weird. But I was just fine with being a weirdo. I'd found my people.

DISCOVERING A WORLD OF STONE

"There's no way I was born to just pay bills and die."

—*Anonymous*

I loved the University of Vermont the moment I got there, in 1977, to major in geography and environmental studies. West of its home in Burlington, the Adirondacks rise from the edge of Lake Champlain. To the east, Mount Mansfield and Camel's Hump bump the sky above the valley below. It is a beautiful place, and I never tired of those views and the changes each season brought.

A little yellow house on the north side of the University Green was home to the UVM Outing Club, and it was one of the first places I visited on campus. The inside was dark and musty, smelling like old sweat and leather, with gear strewn everywhere amidst a few beat-up chairs. Packs and skis, boots and ice axes, ropes and carabiners hung from the walls and spilled out of closets. A sign on the wall announced an introductory rock-climbing course scheduled for the following weekend, inviting students to sign up. I scribbled my name on the sheet. The first week of classes went by in a blur. All I could think about was the coming weekend, when I'd finally get to try the activity I'd read so much about and had long wondered what it was like. A couple years before, in some nearby woods back in New York, I'd discovered a twenty-foot cliff in a local park. The vertical wall had a hand-sized crack, but it was way beyond my ability; I'd managed to get about three feet off the ground before my fear and the climb's difficulty brought me to a screeching halt. Would we be trying the same kind of thing? Was there some kind of magic trick to getting up such walls?

A half dozen or so other kids gathered at the Outing Clubhouse on a cool gray September Saturday. Our instructor, George Biehl, showed up wearing a well-used orange 60/40 parka and gray wool pants, and carrying a small canvas pack. His jacket, with patches sewn on the sleeves proclaiming membership in various climbing and skiing organizations and certification as an EMT, was part of the climber uniform of the time. The shell was a non-insulated blend of nylon and cotton, theoretically woven together tightly enough to repel wind and rain. I'd find, when I eventually purchased one for myself, that the thing failed miserably when put to the test.

George was a handsome man with red hair, a well-groomed mustache, and glasses. Slim and athletic, he looked the part of a climber. George was a chemistry PhD student at UVM, about ten years older than most of us in the group, and had done a little bit of everything. We learned over the course of the day that he was a small-plane pilot, scuba diver, skier, kayaker, mountaineer, and black-belt judo practitioner.

George also excelled at teaching. He was smart, thorough, safe, and—I would learn—had a knack for understanding how to feed information to individuals in almost customized ways they could easily digest. He was a perfect mentor for learning the basics of rock climbing, and over the next year, he would teach me a ton.

A fifteen-minute drive down I-89 from campus took us to a

small trailer park in Bolton Valley. Above the mobile homes rose Bolton Dome, standing high above the Winooski River. This lump of rock crested above the canopy of trees and reached about two hundred feet tall at its highest point. With its somber gray hues framed against the cloudy sky, Bolton Dome looked imposing. I wondered if the other neophytes in our small group felt the same nervousness as me. The cliff revealed itself in more detail once we got to the base: steep walls mixed in with less intimidating, low-angle slabs. The rock type, a schist, had only a few major crack systems. Most of the cliff was dead vertical and looked impossibly smooth, with shiny mica flecks blending in with the otherwise dark stone. The damp woods held the inviting smell of autumn. Some of the maples had turned bright orange and red, while the more stubborn oaks held fast to their green leaves.

George took us to the base of a short, slabby crack about the width of a fist. A discourse on knots was followed by belaying instructions. George kept his cool with a lighthearted smile and laugh as we mangled our figure-eight knots and bowlines until we got them right. None of us owned proper climbing harnesses, nor did the Outing Club supply them. At the time, there were not many commercial climbing harnesses available, and the few that existed were expensive. Most climbers fashioned their own "swami belt" out of two-inch-wide tubular webbing for a waist belt and, for added comfort, sometimes created webbing leg loops as well. But we noobs, just starting out, didn't even own webbing.

Tying a single strand of rope around my waist with a bowline knot, George anchored me with a sling and a locking carabiner to a tree. He then tied into the other end of the rope and arranged his rack—the array of climbing protection—on a sling over his shoulder. George's rack was standard for the era, consisting of carabiners, nylon slings, and variously sized aluminum wedges slung with nylon cord or steel wire, ranging from small slivers the size of a fingernail to large, fist-sized pieces. George called them "stoppers" and "hexentrics," assuring us they would hold fast when placed in the crack, keeping him from hitting the ground if he fell—and if I belayed properly.

I gave George a hip belay, simply wrapping the rope around my waist and slowly letting out slack while he climbed easy terrain, aiming for a ledge about forty feet above. I kept a tight grip on the rope with my "brake hand," the hand responsible for hanging onto the rope should George fall, while simultaneously letting the rope slide through my "guide hand." I had no idea if this belaying stuff actually worked, and I hoped he wasn't going to test my technique. George explained, step-by-step, what he was doing as he climbed. He stopped at little ledges along the way and placed protection in the crack, finding constrictions to slot the odd-shaped aluminum wedges. George then clipped them to the rope with his carabiners, completing the protection link.

At the big ledge, George set up an anchor for the toprope and called for me to take the rope tight. I lowered him to the ground, happy that I had a jacket on—the friction of the rope around my lower back would have given me a painful burn without it. Having now lowered George, I understood that it *was* possible to stop a catastrophe with this simple belaying concept.

Since I'd belayed George, I was the first one to check out the low-angled crack he'd scrambled up. It wasn't at all like that crack in my New York woods. This one looked much easier and much less intimidating. However, I was quickly disabused of thoughts about a casual jaunt. I wore my leather hiking boots, but they scuffed around on the crack and slab, forcing me to weight my arms, which ached by the time I got to the top. George had made the climb look so simple. He did have proper climbing shoes, the era's ubiquitous EB Super Grattons, a. k. a. EBs—smooth-soled rock boots from the French company Edouard Bourdonneau—but there was more to it than that. He knew how to move on the rock, staying in balance and flowing effortlessly, while I was clumsy each step of the way.

After we climbed the first toprope route, George led a couple of us on a short, multi-pitch climb to a higher ledge system, showing us how to string together ropelengths. Tied into the ropes with bowlines-on-a-coil, we followed George up two easy pitches, and then rappelled back to the ground using the traditional Dulfersitz method, in which you run the rope over your back and under your leg. Even through my jacket and pants, the rope cut into my shoulder and crotch with a force I cared not to repeat. After a slightly more difficult toprope route, we made our second rappel of the day, this time with a figure 8 device. Up to that point, we'd just climbed with the rope tied around our waists, but now George created a harness, a thing he called a "Swiss seat," from a long piece of his webbing stash. He threaded the rope through the figure 8, then clipped the 8 to my harness with a locking carabiner. This time, the rappel was a much more comfortable experience.

By the end of the day, I was in love. I was fascinated by the gear and the craft of placing it securely, but I also loved the puzzle of the movement itself—working slowly up a cliffside, figuring out how to move your body, the constant assessment of where to go next. It was art and dance combined with risk management and handling fear. The adrenaline was unlike anything I'd ever experienced. I could see challenges and harder climbs to do all around me. We were outside, on a rock face amidst a lovely wooded hillside, enjoying life. That afternoon, Bolton Dome morphed from imposing giant to an invitation to progression.

George taught us a lot that first day, including the grading system for rock climbs and what it meant to "free climb" a pitch—ascending it without falling, using the rope and gear only for protection in case of a fall, but not for making upward progress. Roped, fifth-class rock climbing started at 5.0 and went as high as 5.11; rumor had it there might even be some 5.12s, somewhere. I asked how hard that day's climbs had been. George said around 5.2 or 5.3, a good place to start as a beginner. I considered how difficult I'd found the climbing. For starters, I had to get some proper footwear.

Maybe the most important information George imparted that day was just how many places there were in the country to rock climb. He talked about places he'd been, from the great walls of Yosemite to the red sandstone of Eldorado Canyon in Colorado, to a place much closer to Burlington—a climbing mecca in New York called the Shawangunks. He even suggested we visit "the Gunks," as climbers called the area, sometime.

I called George a few days later to see if he was serious about a trip to the Shawangunks. He was, and we planned to go on Columbus Day weekend. I went to one of the two outdoor stores in Burlington that carried climbing gear, where I eagerly paged through a little blue guidebook to the Gunks. I couldn't afford to buy the guide along with the other gear I needed, but I was mesmerized by the sheer number of routes and the impossible difficulty of some—one was even graded 5.11! I reflected on George's comment about our Bolton climbs. If those were 5.2 or 5.3, what the hell did a 5.11 offer for holds? Razor blades for the fingers and pinheads for the feet? But first I needed climbing shoes. They didn't have my size in the EBs I so desperately wanted and that George recommended, so I settled instead for a pair of RDs, named for another French alpinist, René Desmaison. The RD was a more heavily built, all-leather shoe that still had the smooth, hard rubber sole all climbing shoes used at the time. I fitted the boots as tightly as I thought appropriate, while wearing a pair of thick wool socks, now barely able to wiggle my toes in the forefoot. I bought a long piece of webbing to craft a Swiss seat harness like George had taught me, something far more comfortable than a single coil of rope around the waist. Another "must have" was a figure 8 device and locking carabiner to avoid any more Dulfersitz rappelling experiences.

George and I, along with another enthusiastic novice, Janie, drove south in my pickup on Saturday, October 8, 1977. George entertained us with stories of his adventures, including his one foray to the Himalayas to climb the trekking summit Island Peak. The day faded from sunny afternoon into colorful dusk, and it was dark when we arrived in New Paltz. We continued through the quiet downtown, crossed the metal bridge over the Wallkill River, and drove west toward the ridge of the Shawangunk Mountains. I could see the outline of the cliffs—a series of elongated lumps on the dark horizon, like giant centipedes resting atop the Earth's surface—but the details of their faces remained invisible in the night.

We parked on a shoulder below the cliffs, and then George marched me and Janie up a trail to a flat spot on top of the Near Trapps, one of the Gunks' main cliffs. We unpacked our sleeping bags and pads on that moonless night, gazing out over the Wallkill Valley, a dark sea of trees that stretched clear to the dim lights of New Paltz.

We woke to crystal-clear skies and to frost coating the tops of our sleeping bags. The autumn foliage was at its colorful best, glowing orange, yellow, and red in the early-morning sun. I looked north and saw the Trapps, the largest cliff in the Gunks, above the road. The flat spot we had slept on was only a few feet from the edge of a 150-foot drop to the talus and trees below. I gazed out on the placid valley, a mix of small fields with barns interspersed with wood lots. The bright-white cliffs stretched north and south of our aerie. The crags were endless! This ridge of immaculate stone went on and on for miles.

I'd found it. This was my place, my cathedral, my home. I knew right then that I would live here, and I couldn't believe I'd grown up a scant eighty miles south of these crags yet had never known they existed. George noted my wide grin and said, "You look like you just woke up on Christmas morning!"

Christmas? Not even a close second to the joy I felt that instant.

We set off to the base of the Near Trapps. George's plan for the day was to lead us up climbs he knew well from previous visits. There were a bunch of climbers on their own routes, and I listened to the jingle of gear and confident belay commands shouted from above. My mood was a mix of nervousness and anticipation. All the climbers we saw looked like they knew what they were doing—they certainly weren't noobies like Janie and me.

George stopped at a near-vertical 5.4 called *Layback* and racked up his gear. I stared up at the route. It looked strenuous—and much steeper, in fact, than the stuff we'd done at Bolton. It started with a short chimney, a wide gap climbed by pressing one's back against one side, and feet against the other, then squirming up the obstacle. At the top of the chimney was a large chockstone lodged in the crack, forming a little roof to climb over before a good rest on a ledge. Then came the real business: the layback section, named for the technique in which you lean sideways off a crack edge and walk your feet up the wall in front of you, maintaining counterpressure.

George stepped onto the rock and moved confidently upward while I belayed, feeding him slack as he climbed. However, I wasn't paying attention to the rope on the ground and suddenly noticed a large, knotted mess at my feet because I hadn't uncoiled the rope carefully enough in my haste to get going. Janie was hurriedly trying to uncoil the cluster as I fed ever-decreasing amounts of untangled rope to George, who was now at the crux layback section and certainly wouldn't have welcomed being pulled off, or "short-roped." Fortunately, an experienced climber walked by and, seeing our predicament, quickly got the cord straightened out, George none the wiser for our little epic. Then our new friend started up our route without a rope, free soloing what George had just led, nonchalantly passing George and continuing to the top. My jaw dropped.

Janie climbed next, struggling a little in the chimney but making it to the belay without a fall. I started up *Layback's* awkward chimney and then muscled my way over the chockstone. Now I stood at a stance below the route's eponymous feature. The cliff steepened here to vertical, and I had to trust my feet as I pressed them against the wall—smearing them on rugosities when there were no edges to stand on. I strained my arms mightily, not really trusting my feet, though my RDs were miles better than my hiking boots and did, in fact, remain glued to the rock. When I got to a good ledge above the crux, I dropped my tired arms and gulped air, realizing I'd barely taken a breath throughout this entire strenuous section. The second pitch, to the top of the cliff, was much easier but spectacular climbing, weaving under large overhangs, taking the line of least resistance.

Janie and I had passed the *Layback* test. George was pleased with us and ready to move on to the next climb. We hiked back down to the base of the cliff, walking past *Layback* to a very steep section of rock that reared past vertical to become overhanging. What was George thinking? He assured us we'd be fine and that *Gelsa*, at 5.4, was allegedly no harder than what we'd already climbed. But I didn't really believe George, and my arms were still tired from the first climb. I didn't understand yet that the rock at the Gunks, because of the way it's stratified, allows climbers to navigate through and around giant overhangs on incut "bucket" holds—ones that sometimes feel as secure as a pullup bar—though I was to get a quick initiation.

Gelsa's first pitch started easily enough, with a long traverse left ending at a perch just big enough for the three of us. I watched George climb the second pitch: a large corner and the steepest section, only stopping every fifteen feet or so to place protection. I knew from George's explanations that any fall would be roughly double the distance he'd climbed above his last piece of protection, and figured he wasn't too worried since he wasn't placing a ton of gear. George went out of view for a time, and eventually we heard his shout from high above: "Off belay!"

Janie climbed, then it was my turn. I looked up at the rope disappearing over the cliff top, some hundred or so feet above me. I tried to not think of how far I had to go, and instead kept my eyes on my immediate surroundings, seeking the edges I needed for feet and hands. The holds were enormous, like climbing a ladder, albeit a very steep ladder. I just kept going, little bit by little bit, forgetting about anything but the next place to put a hand or a foot. I was surprised when I suddenly found myself on top, greeted by the smiling faces of George and Janie. My arms quivered from the effort.

We graduated to a 5.5 called *Disneyland* for our final climb of the day. It was clear this one was going to be more difficult. A slab of rock sheltered by a huge roof featured smaller holds for both hands and feet, and we'd need to use them carefully to get to a little ledge thirty feet above, at the first belay. Beyond that, I had no idea. The route was hidden by the big roof. Some minutes later, Janie and I joined George up at the cramped stance atop pitch one. Overhangs surrounded us, but George weaved around them with total control on the second pitch. I was in awe of his ability to flawlessly and calmly move through such steep terrain. I realized he was climbing well within his limits, reckoning he could only have vague confidence that I would stop any fall with my nascent belay skills, even with the new figure 8.

We bivyed for another night at the same little grassy spot atop the Near Trapps, both Janie and I waking up the next morning tired and sore. George was not afflicted in the least and said we had time to do one more climb before heading back to Burlington.

We walked the carriage road along the Trapps to climb a famous classic 5.5 called *Shockley's Ceiling*. George gave us a quick biography of the first ascensionist, William Shockley. Shockley was just one of the many historically significant characters involved with Gunks climbing who were otherwise known for their more important contributions to the world. In Shockley's case, it was as an inventor of the transistor while working at Bell Labs. Shockley regularly climbed at the Gunks back in the 1950s. I paid scant attention to George's summation of Shockley's life; I was too busy gawking at the puzzle of overhangs, steep corners, and smooth, vertical walls that loomed overhead. *How the hell did climbers pick their way through these obstacles?*

At the base of the route, the ceiling part of *Shockley's Ceiling* was not apparent, and the start looked easy. George led us up the first two pitches. They were confidence-builders and well within my comfort zone. I was happy for that. We sat on the large ledge below the last pitch, where the ceiling had suddenly become all too obvious. The overhang looked difficult, with a hand-sized crack running up to its three-foot length. This overhang was much bigger than anything we'd done so far. Janie and I tried not to show our concern, but George sensed our intimidation and reassured us that we'd be fine. "Just watch what I do," George explained. "You'll see where I can use a hand jam and a heel hook at the lip of the overhang to help you get over the top."

His easy flow and banter while climbing the ceiling, pointing out the holds and how to use them, relaxed me a tad—until Janie went next and almost fell. Fortunately, George had placed a long sling at the lip of the overhang for us to step into if we couldn't free-climb the crux. Janie grabbed the sling and got a foot into it, allowing her to step over the roof. Now I was nervous. We hadn't fallen or resorted to pulling on gear the day before. When George called for me to climb, I disassembled the belay, felt the rope come taut on my waist, and tried to calm my nerves by focusing only on the holds in front of me. I called to George, "Climbing!" and zeroed in on the features he'd pointed out, remembering to carefully place my feet on the best ones. It worked! I stood over the roof on good holds, breathing hard, relieved to have made it.

On the drive home to Vermont, I peppered George with questions about the Gunks. He'd brought the 1972 edition of the guidebook with us, the blue one I'd seen at the gear shop. Between climbs, I'd studied the little book, unaware of how out of date it was now, in 1977. I would soon learn the bar for difficulty in the Gunks had risen exponentially since its publication.

The hardest climb we'd done was 5.5. What was a 5.8 like? The hardest climb George had ever led was 5.7. The one 5.11 in the guide was called *Doug's Roof*. George pointed it out as we made our way to *Shockley's Ceiling*. While only fifteen feet or so off the ground, the six-foot overhang itself looked featureless to me. What kind of mutant could climb something like that? I returned to the shop after our trip to buy the guide, but it was gone—out of print, none available to order, I was told. Still, this didn't stop the dreams of more climbing in the Gunks. I couldn't wait to return.

Back at UVM, I ferreted out experienced climbing partners through the Outing Club. There weren't a lot, but I could usually find someone to hit a local crag after class. Besides Bolton, there was the even-more-accessible Winooski railroad cut, just a ten-minute drive from campus and a local resource a small crew of us used several times a week. The tiny "Cut" was exactly that: a thirty-foot-high, fifty-yard-wide slash of dolomite blasted out of a hillside above the Winooski River to make a path for trains. The train operators knew of our presence and would blow their horns well in advance of coming through the notch so we'd have time to move our ropes—and selves—off the tracks. We squeezed against the wall while the train slowly chugged through. The engineer always gave a wave, just a few feet from our noses.

What the dynamite-blasted wall lacked in aesthetics, it made up for with the ease of access and quick toprope setups. I was able to do a couple routes on the vertical face without too much trouble, but most of the climbs took me multiple trips to complete. The holds tended to be small and slick, requiring finger power to link moves. The Cut demanded I learn how to more effectively use my feet and more powerfully crimp my fingers on the tiny edges, curling them over and closing the grip with my thumb. Between the railroad cut and Bolton, the remainder of the fall saw me out every chance I got. By the time the last of the colorful autumn leaves hit the ground, the calluses on my fingertips were thick as nickels.

Winter came to Burlington quickly, and rock climbing came to a halt. But George had a plan for spring break in 1978. He herded together a group of Outing Club climbers for a visit to West Virginia's Seneca Rocks. Besides the Gunks, Seneca was "the other" place to climb in the Mid-Atlantic, and being much farther south, it would have better weather in early April. We piled the gang and gear into my pickup and made the long drive down from Vermont.

The hamlet of Seneca was in the middle of nowhere, a simple intersection of a couple two-lane roads and two general stores, one of which doubled as a gas station. The Yokums owned one store, the Harpers the other one. I expected to see Li'l Abner pop out of a doorway at any moment.

Seneca Rocks itself erupts from a steep hillside above the tiny town as a giant fin of quartzite. It looks like the back of a stegosaurus, with two main summits and a phalanx of small spires protruding from its spine. This fin provides a great benefit by having two sides to climb on—the East and West faces—which lets you choose either sun or shade.

We walked into Harper's store to see what it offered. The usual Seneca Rocks climber crowd mostly came from the D.C.

Seneca Rocks, 1978

and Pittsburgh areas, and the shop folks were surprised to see Vermonters. The shop's single large room was dimly lit, with shelves of groceries and basic household products. In one corner, an ancient woman sat in her rocking chair, dressed in a long drab gown with a blanket wrapped over her shoulders. She slowly rocked back and forth, in synch with her singing:

"The old gray mare, she ain't what she used to be,

Ain't what she used to be, ain't what she used to be.

The old gray mare, she ain't what she used to be,

Many long years ago."

Buck Harper, the shop's owner, extended his hand to greet me, exclaiming he wanted to give a proper welcome with his "West Virginia handshake." He tightly gripped my hand and yanked with all his might, pulling me into his chest. I didn't know how to react; my shoulder stung from the force, but Buck laughed his ass off. I gave a forced smile and decided it might be a better idea to shop at Yokums'.

There was a surprisingly good gear shop in town, the Gendarme, which stocked all the newest climbing gizmos and seemed to be the only place in the hamlet with a hint of modernity. The shop was named for a rock feature, the most significant spire on the Seneca Rock formation, a popular mini-summit with a "must-do" 5.4 for every climber who visited. The thirty-foot quartzite obelisk sat squarely in the middle of a depression on the ridge, aptly called Gunsight Notch.

John Markwell, the shop's proprietor, was a font of useful information about the complex cliff: the best approaches, where to camp, and, most importantly, how to avoid pissing off the locals by trespassing onto their properties. We crossed the footbridge over the North Fork of the South Branch of the Potomac River from the dirt parking lot and set up camp on one of the few flat spots below the rock, ferrying loads to our hillside village.

Our assumption of good weather proved wrong. The West Virginia mountains do not dole out sunshine without a fight, especially in early spring. Showers over the first couple of days gave us ample time to experience all the amenities town had to offer, meaning we mostly hung out in the gear shop fondling stuff we couldn't afford to buy. When the cold rain finally stopped, everyone exploded in a burst of pent-up energy. George and I charged up the muddy hillside and scrambled up some ledges to the base of a formation named Humphrey's Head. I wanted to do my first lead on the 5.3 that attained the little summit, which stood forty feet above our perch. That rig had my name all over it. 5.3 stood well within my wheelhouse for an easy introduction to the sharp—lead climber's—end of the rope.

If Humphrey's actual head looked anything like this formation—with its protruding nose, bulbous forehead, and receding chin, all smacking of serious inbreeding—he had my sympathy. Perhaps Humphrey could read my unkind thoughts as I racked up and tied in, and decided he wasn't gonna take no shit from some yankee.

The climb was a little less than vertical, and the holds were obvious, though still soggy from the monsoonal drenchings. I climbed a few feet up, to the base of a small bulge, and worked to place a wired nut in a shallow crack. The nut wasn't cooperating, but eventually it stayed put when I tugged on it. I clipped the rope to the piece and started moving up. As soon as I weighted my foot, it slipped, and I lost my grip on the slick handholds. The dubious nut popped out of the crack, smacking me in the chest as soon as my weight hit it. I cratered on the ledge right next to George, landing on my ass with the slack rope piled on top of me.

My very first lead attempt had resulted in a five-foot groundfall. Even as short as the fall was, I'd broken the most basic tenet in climbing: don't hit the ground! George gave me a concerned look that turned to a chuckle once he saw I was fine, aside from being extremely embarrassed. He offered to take over. "No way," I said. I paid more attention to the holds on my second attempt, careful to use only the driest ones and finishing the route—but not before Humphrey had had a good laugh at my expense.

MY NEW BACKYARD IN THE GUNKS

"Don't be afraid to fail. Be afraid not to try."

—Michael Jordan

While I visited home for winter break after my first autumn of climbing, my mother said, "I was talking with Aunt Florence today. Did you know your cousin Danny is a rock climber?"

Danny, my mother's first cousin, was about eight years my senior and lived in New Jersey. As a young boy, I was on his heels when we were together at sporadic family gatherings, but my memory of Danny was vague—I hadn't talked to him nor seen him since I was a little kid.

I immediately called him up. He was just as surprised as I that we shared a love of rock climbing. We planned to get together in the Gunks when spring arrived. Danny told me he climbed up there all the time. When I got off the phone, I couldn't wait for the next season. I had a partner for the Gunks, and it was someone who knew the area well.

When spring arrived, Danny and I met at the Gunks. I found myself freshly besotted with the place. One of the great attributes of the Gunks is how friendly the rock is for climbing, like it was created just for those wanting to scale the bluffs. While there are plenty of large, intimidating overhangs, the abundance of horizontal cracks makes the climbing feel very natural, like playing on a jungle gym. In the Gunks, what separates hard from easy routes are the distances between those horizontals, the size of the holds, and how many overhangs a climb contains.

Danny and I forged a partnership, and he introduced me to the other regulars, climbers I'd get to know well since they were there religiously every weekend. Danny was a much better, more experienced climber than me, having started several years earlier. He had huge, vein-laced forearms, disproportional to his biceps, which were impressive enough in themselves. While shorter than me by several inches, he was much more muscular. His dark-brown thatch of hair came down off his forehead to thick black eyebrows and brown eyes. He looked like he could beat the shit out of an oak tree—the kind of guy you'd want on your side in a bar fight.

Danny and I developed a ritual. On weekend mornings, we met at the Uberfall, a small section of the Trapps by the road where a spring provided water for canteen filling and a convenient place for the climbing community to congregate. The scene was a fun mélange of testosterone, hyperbole, and general bullshitting. A coffin-sized box at the base of a low overhang contained rescue gear in the event of a climbing accident, but mostly it served as a bench. Climbers teamed up for routes they'd planned during the week. Gear got sorted, packs were filled, and then the climbers left two by two, only to be seen again at the day's end to report on their grand accomplishments or make excuses for their failures.

Early in our partnership, Danny led the hardest pitches, while I took the lead on some of the easier ones. Danny's mentoring helped my climbing progress rapidly. With George, everything had been about safety. With Danny, progression was the name of the game, working our way up the grade ladder. Danny didn't abandon safety, but he pushed a lot harder. He was willing to take falls while he led—short, safe ones at least. His efforts pushed me to try harder as well.

One Saturday, Danny already had the plan for our morning. The prior weekend, he had followed another climber up *Fat Stick Direct*, a 5.9 in the Near Trapps. He had no problem seconding the pitch, which he said had good gear, and now he wanted to lead it. 5.9 was a serious grade in the Gunks, and *Fat Stick Direct* was reputed to be difficult for the grade, on a scale that went up, I'd since learned, to 5.12 at the time. There were very few 5.12 climbs anywhere in 1978, and those in the Gunks had only been climbed by a select group of superhumans who'd made a deal with the devil. 5.9, by most any climber's standard then, meant damn hard. At that point, the hardest I had climbed, seconding Danny, was 5.8.

Fat Stick Direct had three short pitches, each about sixty feet long. Danny offered me the first pitch, a 5.7, but I declined. I wasn't warmed up and I had butterflies in my belly already, thinking about the crux second pitch. Danny led up easily and put me on belay. I climbed poorly while seconding, pumping out my forearms from nervously over-gripping the holds and muscling my way through moves that would have easily yielded to finesse.

"Well, that was pretty strenuous," I said at the belay anchor. Danny just looked at me and smirked. I could see he was thinking, *"If you think THAT was hard, just wait."*

Danny re-racked the gear, arranging the nuts neatly on his gear sling in the order in which he would place them, all while looking up at the crux—a small overhang leading into a short corner above. I shifted around to get in the best position to arrest a potential fall, orienting myself with Danny's line of ascent. With an, "Okay, climbing," Danny set off, arriving at the business in short order and only a few yards away from me. He reached through the overhang. I couldn't tell what he was grabbing, but I could see his feet scraping around for purchase and hear his grunts of effort as he battled through the crux. After a victory whoop and a short rest at a stance above, Danny sprinted up easier terrain above the corner. Soon, I heard his call: "Off belay!"

My heart was in overdrive while I disassembled the belay station. At the crux, I yarded with all I had to clear the overhang. Though I was out of his sightline, Danny could feel my progress as he took in rope and shouted encouragement: "Yeah, yeah, keep moving!" I soon stood next to my cousin on a small belay ledge, having seconded the crux pitch without falling. I panted as if I'd just run a four-minute mile. It was Danny's hardest lead to date, and the hardest climb I'd done, period. We thought ourselves to be pretty badass.

Danny racked up again and started leading the final pitch. Not far above me, he clipped the rope into an ancient piton, a steel relic hammered into the rock and left behind decades earlier, now slowly rusting in place. He climbed smoothly on the easy terrain, and I lost sight of him after he disappeared around an overhang.

Suddenly, Danny screamed something; I couldn't tell what, but it was loud. He climbed faster now, and I had trouble paying out slack to match his speed. He was still yelling, and then he bellowed a sound that was downright primordial—something from deep inside the reptilian cortex. I realized something was terribly wrong.

Just then, I heard the "thunk" of a block of stone hitting the

Russ on "Arrow" in the Gunks, circa 1978

cliff above, then falling to the ground below. Following close behind, my cousin plummeted toward me. Danny's eyes bugged out as he fell past the belay, still screaming. I'll never forget the look on his face, and I am sure he won't forget mine. Danny had upset a large wasp nest, hence the rapid climbing and shouting as they stung him. The loose block was something he would have avoided under normal circumstances, but he had been careless while racing to escape the attack.

As Danny sailed by, a small cloud of pissed-off wasps followed in his wake. I squeezed my eyes shut and got ready for the impact, my brake hand death-gripped on the rope. I'd never held a lead fall of any real consequence before—just short, little ones. Danny's sixty-footer was to be a hell of an initiation.

I felt the jolt on my belay device and the sharp tug upward as the force of the fall hit me. The impact was massive, but everything held: the belay anchor, the directional nuts for an upward pull he'd placed at the start of the pitch, and even that ancient museum piece of a piton, the lone piece of downward-pulling gear between Danny and me. Danny hung below an overhang, out of sight. "Danny! Are you okay?!" I shouted. I held fast to the rope and watched Danny re-emerge, hand-over-handing up the rope, feet not even touching the rock and repeating mantra-like, "I broke my arm, I broke my arm, I broke my arm . . ."

He reached the belay, and I clipped him in. The damnable wasps had followed Danny back to the belay, and we waved our arms and whirled our slings in the air to fight them off. They relented, but not before Danny got an extra couple stings. I suggested to Danny that he likely hadn't broken his arm, since he now had the unofficial rope-climbing speed record. But he *was* banged up, his elbow swollen to the size of a cantaloupe and his face, arms, and legs covered in welts. Danny also complained that his hip hurt. We were assessing our next steps when, from the overlook parking area on the main road, we heard somebody yell, "DO YOU NEED A RESCUE?!" Apparently, our antics had not gone unnoticed. We shouted back, in unison, "NO!!!" We weren't far off the ground—we could manage.

"Danny," I said, "the best thing is to just lower you to the ground, and I'll leave some gear in at the belay and rap down. You cool with that?"

"Yeah, let's get outta here," he said.

I started to lower him, but then, as he got about twenty feet below me, with the rope running over terrain we hadn't climbed on our ascent, his screaming started anew. Danny Batmanned up the rope again, followed by another gang of wasps, using him like a pincushion. He'd disturbed another nest as I lowered him. I started twirling the sling around my head immediately to preemptively ward off the angry insects.

Back at the belay, Danny did not look well. He'd lost some color, and I was afraid he was going into shock. As we discussed our next move, we were suddenly beset by another wasp attack, this time from above. Our would-be rescuers had watched our unfortunate efforts thus far and decided, despite our previous declaration, that we needed help. As they lowered a rope to extract us, it ran straight through the nest above—the one Danny had originally disturbed.

"GET THAT FUCKING ROPE OUTTA HERE!!!" I yelled. Slowly, the rope snaked back up the cliff. Danny and I could rescue ourselves. I suggested lowering him again, but this time with a directional nut to put him right over our line of ascent; we hadn't

Russ on the ever-popular boulder problem, "Gill Egg," circa 1979

encountered any wasps on the way up the route to our present belay.

"No way," he declared. "You should lead us out of here on the last pitch of *Yellow Ridge*."

Yellow Ridge was a moderately easy 5.6, but my nerves were shot. Still, it was the only option besides my nixed plan of lowering off, so I started climbing. The pitch to the top traversed left and up. As I led out, I placed gear frequently, worrying about Danny's condition and ability to catch me if I fell.

About halfway along the pitch, I saw it: another "Death Star" wasp nest the size of a softball, right above a piton I needed to clip. I approached slowly, seeing a couple sentry wasps waggling their wings in warning. I stayed as far below the piton as I could, pressed a carabiner up to clip it, and snuck past. On top, I tied into an oak tree to belay. As I pulled in slack while Danny climbed,

Jack Mileski (preparing to celebrate the end of the climbing day) with Doug Strickholm and Danny Costa, circa 1978

I heard another yell. He'd reached the wasp-nest piton and had been stung again, taking a swinging fall. Once the pendulum stopped, he arm-over-armed his way up the rope in a reprise of his earlier gymnastics, putting his large biceps to good use and providing irrefutable evidence that his arm wasn't busted.

We got back to our cars, and I took Danny to the emergency room. He had a badly bruised hip, a severe contusion on his arm, lots of scrapes, and uncountable wasp stings. Amazingly, nothing was broken, and the ER doctor was impressed Danny hadn't gone into anaphylactic shock from all that venom.

With Danny out of commission for a few weeks, I needed a new partner. Though the overall vibe at the Gunks was friendly, there was a pecking order—and finding my way through it took some observation. The easiest way to assess others' skills was to watch climbers in the Uberfall area; it was always busy on the weekends, especially at the start and end of the day. I could see who did what boulder problems and which climbs, and judge if those climbers looked solid or sketchy. It didn't take too long to figure out who was who.

At the top of the pyramid were the *emeriti,* made up of a very few individuals like Fritz Wiessner, Hans Kraus, and Jim McCarthy. Wiessner and Kraus were the originals, the first rock climbers in the Gunks and ascensionists of many of the most popular climbs. Wiessner emigrated from the Saxony area of Germany in 1929 and had earned his chops on the sandstone towers of Elbsandstein, where he'd free-climbed at a high standard. Kraus, also an émigré, came from Austria, and his skills had been honed in the Dolomites, where he happily resorted to aid climbing to get to the top of those big walls. Kraus and his family fled Europe for the States in 1938.

The climbs, done in the 1930s and '40s by this pair, were difficult for the time and remained classic "must dos," though they were no longer considered challenging. Kraus' masterpiece *High Exposure* is 5.6, which in 1941, was pretty hard. Today, many climbers still find the climb unnerving, as it forces the climber to step out over a 150-foot void to clear an overhang guarding the slightly overhanging, but very exposed, upper face. Wiessner was a master free climber. His hardest creation in the Gunks is a climb at Sky Top named *Minnie Belle*. It's a wide crack, rated 5.8 and done in 1946, and at the time, was unprotectable in its crux section—Wiessner essentially free-soloed it. *Minnie Belle* remained the hardest climb in the Gunks for years, but for Wiessner, it was far from his hardest climb. Some of the routes he'd done on his home turf in Germany would have been rated at least 5.9 and were many years ahead of their time.

The "McCarthy Era" came after Wiessner and Kraus, and he and his partners pushed standards in free climbing to a new high—5.10 in the late 1950s and early '60s. Even in the late 1970s, McCarthy's routes were still considered tests of skill, boldness, and strength. Jim's routes defined his era, and his prowess allowed him to break through barriers on climbs like *M.F.* (5.9), *Never Never Land* (5.10), and *Tough Shift* (5.10 and trouser-filling scary, pulling insecure moves way out from protection). There was no skipping McCarthy climbs as we ascended the ladder of difficulty.

These elder silverbacks weren't climbing hard any longer by the day's standards, but they were legends and could still be seen around the crag. McCarthy was a regular weekender, but Fritz and Hans were a rarer sighting, like spotting a species of migrating bird at your feeder. Everyone knew who they were and greeted them reverently.

Beneath the *emeriti* came the *demi-gods*, the "Prophets of Purism," as they were sometimes called for their strict adherence to the proper "rules" of traditional free climbing style. This "Gang of Four"—John Stannard, Steve Wunsch, John Bragg, and Henry Barber—brought the Gunks to the forefront of free climbing in the early 1970s. They led the way not just in the Gunks, but in the world, by sticking to what it meant to "properly" climb a route: using only the natural holds on the rock, no weighting the rope or gear, and always starting from the bottom without any knowledge of what lay ahead (today, this is called "*onsight* climbing"). If you fell, you immediately returned to the ground or belay stance. Hanging on the rope and continuing, something that would later earn the derisive name "hangdogging," was a disqualification of a legitimate ascent, as would be toproping prior to a lead attempt. The one allowance was that you could leave the rope attached to the highest piece of protection after a fall. This "yo-yo" style was the essence of purity in the 1970s, though, of course, the next climber got to essentially toprope to the high point on his try, and you could push the toprope ever higher until it was rigged for nearly the entire pitch.

John Stannard was a physicist and looked every bit the part, wearing glasses and a serious countenance. Around six feet tall, he had long arms, long, skinny legs, and a V-shaped torso, all of which served him well on the overhangs in the Gunks. Stannard viewed the Gunks as an area for free-climbing and considered aid to be foul play. His reasoning made sense. Any buffoon could engineer their way to the top of a two-hundred-foot cliff by pulling on the rope and gear. What kind of challenge is that?

Free-climbing was all about solving the puzzle presented by the rock's natural holds—its cracks and edges with which you communed to create a dance with the rock. John was not afraid to lay siege to a climb that was too hard for him at first, to fail attempt after attempt, weekend after weekend, until he eventually succeeded. John's persistence was second to none—he had no quit in him. One of his best routes is *Persistent*, an aptly named, severely overhanging 5.11+ finger crack he spent many weekends on before mastering.

In 1972, Dick Williams published the blue-covered edition of the Shawangunk guidebook, including routes that used aid to bypass difficult spots. Stannard didn't like this, so he decided to do something about it. John led the charge in 1973, recruiting his able ropemates to eliminate the aid from all thirty-eight aid climbs listed in the new publication. By the end of the year, the Gang of Four had free-climbed thirty-three of those routes, leaving only five with aid—an amazing accomplishment in just a year's time.

Some of the freed routes were relatively straightforward, with only a few aid moves to conquer, but others lived in a distant, more complex zip code. Now as free climbs, routes like *Kansas City* (5.12), *To Have or Have Not* (5.12), *The Throne* (5.12), *Yellow Wall* (5.11), and *Kligfield's Follies* (5.11+) created quite the trophy case of accomplishments. Not only were these climbs difficult, but some had sparse protection and demanded serious boldness and a calm head. The push in free-climbing standards continued into the following year, and in 1974 Wunsch climbed the severely overhanging fissure of *Supercrack* at Sky Top. Given a proposed grade of 5.13 (it later settled at 5.12+), *Supercrack* was widely regarded as the hardest climb yet done in the Gunks and maybe the most difficult single-pitch route in the world.

By 1974, due to the free-climbing onslaught of Stannard et al., the Gunks held one of the world's hardest collections of free climbs—arguably *the* hardest. The thing is, it wasn't well known, and the grades of many routes remained shrouded in mystery, since 5.12 had yet to be codified in any guidebooks, anywhere. The depth of the accomplishment by Stannard and company would not be understood for years, until other talented visitors tried these climbs. In the mid- to late-1970s, there were three major rock-climbing centers in the United States: in the East, it was the Shawangunks; in the Rockies, it was the Boulder, Colorado, area; and in the West, Yosemite was the mecca. In the mid-seventies, the Gunks had a harder collection of free climbs than either of the others.

The "Prophets of Purism" also led the way on another front, trading in their pitons and hammers for early iterations of passive protection, which could be placed without a hammer. Climbers had come to notice that the continuous pounding of hard steel pitons into and out of cracks badly altered the rock on popular climbs, breaking away the lip of the rock and leaving permanent "pin scars." In the United States, piggybacking off a movement in England, climbers had begun slowly phasing in "chocks" and "nuts" instead. But in the Gunks, it became a religious conversion. This new protection consisted of aluminum wedges of various shapes and sizes that fit into natural constrictions. Stannard and his partners fully embraced the "clean climbing" ethic in its nascent stages. The fact that the best climbers in the area gave up their pitons on the hardest routes yet done anywhere encouraged all Gunks climbers to discontinue hammering pitons into the rock. Along with the banishment of pitons was the prohibition against using bolts. Very few bolts existed in the Gunks anyway, and their use had always been frowned upon—a nod to the need for boldness.

Stannard even went so far as to fashion his own pitons, made of softer steel, to leave fixed on the older classic routes that would, at the time, have been poorly protected with existing, "clean climbing" gear. To create even more buzz for the movement, Stannard also started a logbook at the local climbing shop, Rock & Snow, for all to record their "first clean ascents" of routes that had heretofore utilized pitons.

When I showed up in the Gunks, Stannard's hardest climbing days were behind him, but he still climbed at an extremely high level and often traveled to the Gunks from his home in the Washington, D.C., area. Wunsch remained an impressive climber when he got out, but he'd become more focused on business and financial markets than the cliffs. Bragg was still in the midst of his powers, having just done his new route, *Gravity's Rainbow*, a stiff 5.12 at Lost City. Barber was also still climbing difficult routes, but he wasn't regularly hanging out in the Gunks, instead exporting his purist style to cliffs around the world on his global travels.

Underneath the upper echelons, a younger generation of climbers occupied the next ladder rung down. This large group spent their time gunning for what they called the "first human ascents" of the routes the Stannard posse had pioneered, as well as opening their own new climbs. They were good climbers, the best of the late seventies, and could often be found climbing together. It wasn't unusual to see them assembled, four to seven strong, taking turns inching their rope up a difficult project, yo-yo style.

Below these higher castes lay just about everyone else who enthusiastically climbed every weekend—including myself.

Experience varied, so the trick was to pick a partner who was roughly of the same ability level or had an interest in the same route. At the Uberfall, I noticed a couple of prospective partners. One fellow was fit looking and always wore white martial arts pants and a white T-shirt, all of which gave him an air of climbing hard, though I actually had no idea. His name was Mike Burlingame and he lived in New Jersey. His partner was a little younger, and I knew he climbed around the same grade as me since I'd seen him on a few climbs. He was Rich Strang. Rich lived on Long Island, a detail that was impossible to miss given his strong accent. Both Mike and Rich knew my cousin Danny a little, and like everyone else in the Gunks, they'd heard about his giant fall on *Fat Stick* and the ensuing rescue misadventure.

One day in that late spring of 1978, the three of us partnered up for a test run. Mike decided our first climb together would be a 5.10 called *Transcontinental Freeway*, a Jim McCarthy testpiece—a difficult, benchmark climb he'd established in 1965. It wouldn't have been my pick—I'd never climbed a 5.10 before—but I didn't want to back down.

We got to the base of the climb, which starts with a difficult move over a bulge before weaving up steep, obtuse dihedrals, and started sorting our rack. In our quiet preparation, we all mulled silently over the obvious, unspoken-so-far question: *Who would lead this thing?*

It was an awkward moment. None of us approached the uncoiled rope at the foot of the route to tie into the lead end. Mike broke the ice: "Hey, Russ—you wanna lead?" he asked. Apparently, he was under the impression that I was some kind of expert—a hardman—who had already climbed 5.10.

"Mike," I said, "I hate to break it to you, but I've never climbed a 5.10. I thought maybe *you* had!"

"Well, I've done a bunch of 5.9s, but this is my first one," responded Mike, and we all had a nervous laugh.

It turned out we were all climbing around 5.9 and looking to break into harder grades. Rich and I eventually coaxed Mike to go for it, as we deemed him the most likely to succeed. After all, he had the cool karate pants.

Mike looked nervous while he tied in. *Transcon*, as it's familiarly called, was not one of the Stannard mystery routes but rather a well-known climb, frequently done by the best climbers. We had a good idea of how hard it would be and where the cruxes were. We also knew it was a reasonably safe, well-protected route, with ample gear-placement opportunities along its length.

Mike climbed a short section of easy rock to a ledge. He stood there for a few minutes, placing a couple of nuts to back up an old fixed piton—badly bent from past hammerings—in its shallow vertical crack. Then Mike stepped up, made the first hard move past the piton, and promptly fired the pitch. Rich and I had been prepared for a more typical yo-yo style siege, but Burlingame cruised *Transcon*, pausing briefly at the cruxes and placing solid gear before pulling through each one. Rich went next, using the same sequence of moves Mike had unlocked; the holds were obvious, covered in white gymnastic chalk from the many hands that had grabbed them recently. Rich also made it up without a fall. It was my turn now, and the pressure was on. I stuffed my feet into my climbing shoes, a pair of new, as-yet-unworn RR Varapes—another imported European rock boot. They were supposed to be a major upgrade from my bulky, insensitive, and too-large RDs. I'd fitted these new shoes painfully tight, and this time without wearing socks. When I'd put them on at the shop, my toes had gone numb after a few minutes. It seemed a small price to pay for higher performance, plus the rubber on the soles was noticeably softer than on my RDs.

I mimicked the sequence I'd watched Mike and Rich use on the tricky first crux. My feet felt secure on the small holds—the new shoes were indeed painful, but they worked—and I soon found myself at the next crux, a two-foot overhang. The handholds were big, and I muscled through to a good rest. After a breather, I climbed the dihedrals to join Rich and Mike on our perch. I had followed the pitch without a fall, pleasantly surprised to have my first Gunks 5.10 under my belt.

With that success, we wondered about the newer free climbs. How hard were they, really? Hanging around the Uberfall, we'd heard some of the better climbers talking about a handful of those routes, piquing our interest. We would soon find out through trial and error that some of the climbs were, in fact, within our ability, while others lay far outside our grasp. But we had to explore for ourselves—it was part of the Gunks ethos. The climbers in the upper tiers considered it good sport to let us lesser climbers get in over our heads and scare ourselves shitless. In fact, it would have been the height of presumptuousness, a rupture of the chain of command, to solicit the Stannard-era pioneers for info on these climbs.

The one exception to this rule was Kevin Bein. Kevin was a talented and gregarious soul, a barrel-chested ball of energy who had been in the scene since the 1960s. He climbed often with the Stannard gang, and easily shape-shifted into the following generations as well. Kevin was everybody's best friend, known as the "Mayor of the Gunks," always happy to help and give important beta—blow-by-blow information—about crux moves and protection. And most crucially, I could count on him not trying to kill us with bullshit information about the unknown routes. Kevin was the bridge between us and the leading climbers of the day, often joining us lesser mortals on our projects and keeping us safe.

WESTWARD HA! A ROAD TRIP FOR ROCK AND ROMANCE

"When you come to a fork in the road, take it."

—*Yogi Berra*

I made plans to go west, in the summer of 1979, with my friend Mike Young. We'd done a bunch of ice climbing together the previous winter and got along well. He was a medical student at UVM and part of the small circle of climbers in the Burlington area. Mike was older than me by six or seven years and a big guy, well over six feet tall. He had an angular face with a strong jawline and a thick mop of curly brown hair. When dressed in his ice-climber outfit of wool knickers, knee socks, and heavy sweater, Mike looked every bit the Norman Rockwell caricature of a mountaineer.

I couldn't wait to explore the places out west I'd only read about. Mike and I had agreed it would be a mountain trip, focusing on the Tetons and the Wind River Range in Wyoming. That had all sounded great when we'd planned the trip during the winter, but now, on the eve of our departure, I was unsure that was what I really wanted to do. My attention was one hundred percent on rock climbing and doing ever-more difficult routes, not on long, moderate alpine climbs. Still, I had committed to the trip and the plan, so off we went. When we started our drive, I suggested we stop at a couple of rock venues en route to break up the drive. Mike was game, if we didn't spend too much time diverted from our main agenda. The Needles of South Dakota, a beetling of granite domes and spires in the Black Hills near Mount Rushmore, were first on the list.

The early-morning sun draped the South Dakota badlands in a soft glow as we cruised into the western edge of the state. The Black Hills rose in front of us, heralding our departure from the monotonous flatlands. We found a campsite in Custer State Park and gaped at the spires around us that popped up over the evergreens. Sylvan Lake, in the heart of the park, was a fairy-tale setting, a dark jewel in a pine forest with lumpy towers of stone stretching into an azure sky. I walked over to a large boulder and touched it, feeling the texture of the stone. The knobby crystals in the rock were inviting, holds big and small scattered everywhere.

As a warm-up climb to the area after our all-night drive, we picked an easy-looking 5.7 spire from the guidebook. Immediately, I got a lesson in the deceptive nature of the Needles. The abundance of protruding crystals gave me a ton of choices about where to climb, but picking the right way—route-finding— was crucial. Finding the easiest, 5.7 path was tricky, and since it was pure face climbing without cracks to wriggle protection into— and in-situ bolts and pitons had been placed only sparingly—the climb demanded a cool head and patience. After a few false starts and dead ends, I got to the top of the spire, having worked hard for a measly 5.7.

We spent the next few days on classic routes on these small towers that somehow always felt bigger when I was leading them. Even though the climbs were frightening and sometimes downright dangerous because of their lengthy runouts between protection, the towers were amazingly fun to climb, as was recording our ascents in the small summit registers. Some towers had no fixed rappel anchor, so we would simul-rappel back to the ground, one of us sliding down the rope on one side of the tower while the other slid down the opposite side, the rope precariously secured in a depression atop the pinnacle. Communication and timing were important: if one of us got to the ground before the other and unweighted the rope, the unfortunate one opposite would suddenly be in a free fall.

Next stop on my list was Devils Tower in Wyoming. Whereas the Needles tested my knack for route-finding, the Tower required nothing of the sort. The routes were all well-protected volcanic cracks, soaring straight up six hundred feet in plumb lines to the summit. We simply needed to pick a grade and a size of crack that suited our fingers and hands, and then climb away. I loved the climbing, but Mike clearly wasn't enjoying it nearly as much. He didn't outright say anything negative, but I knew his moods well enough to know he was biding his time. After just a couple days at the Tower, we moved on and settled into a campsite at the American Alpine Club's Grand Teton Climbers' Ranch. Now that we were in the Tetons, in the real mountains, Mike came alive. His smile was ear-to-ear, and his eyes lit up when he peered up at the peaks.

The Tetons were a beautiful sight from the valley. The rocky peaks were festooned with jumbled buttresses of stone and patches of snow. Mike and I climbed a few multi-pitch rock routes the first couple of days. The climbs were considered classics of the area, but I found them uninspiring. An aspect of rock routes I find compelling is an obvious line of ascent: features that grab me, demanding to be climbed. These can be soaring crack lines, bordered by smooth, unblemished stone; or a corner system defining the obvious, only, logical way up. It may even be just a series of chalk-dusted holds on a bolted limestone wall. But in the Tetons, it was all chaos to my eye—it looked like we could climb just about anywhere. Most of the time, I didn't see the lines, aside from how they were described in the guidebook. Mike looked up and saw beautiful climbs; I saw only entropy.

We usually had to hike quite a way just to get to the routes—we were doing a lot more approaching than climbing. So while I quickly grew tired of the place, Mike climbed better and harder here than he had in the Needles or at Devils Tower. In fact, he even seemed to appreciate the long approaches and route-finding challenges.

We geared up for a climb of the Grand Teton. Mike was psyched to do the *Black Ice Couloir*, a lengthy ice climb up the north side of the mountain. We hiked up the long trail of never-ending switchbacks to the saddle on the Grand's north side, finding a comfortable notch where we could bivouac for the night.

At first light, we traversed along a ledge system until we came to a snowy couloir. Mike checked our guidebook and determined we were at the start of our climb. He took the first pitch, an easy snow gully. I took the next pitch. It was more of the same: low-angle ice with some snow patches. When Mike joined me at the belay, I asked, "Isn't this thing supposed to be kinda hard?" The *Black Ice Couloir* was described in the guidebook as a sixty-degree runnel with some steeper sections. The route so far had been an easy outing up a snow trough, and didn't look to get any harder as we got higher. In the end, back at the campground, we learned from some other climbers that we'd done the wrong climb; we hadn't traversed far enough on the ledge system to reach the *Black*

Ice Couloir and had instead climbed the *Enclosure Couloir,* a much simpler affair. It didn't matter to me. I hadn't found our climb fun in the least. I began counting the days until we could leave.

Both Mike and I got lucky when another UVM friend, Gordon Banks, arrived. Gordon lived in Colorado and was one of my climbing partners at UVM. I enjoyed climbing with him whenever we tied in together. Gordon had an easy, quiet way that countered my more brash and sometimes raspy manner. He never got flustered, as far as I could tell, and that quiet disposition allowed him to rationally calculate his way through situations without going over the top. We once got caught in a sudden thunderstorm atop a summit at Seneca Rocks. I was freaking out, trying to get the rope set for a rappel. The rope was whipping in the wind and getting stuck on protrusions while I tried to even out the ends to get us down. While I tugged and cursed, Gordon patiently coaxed the rope into place without a sound, and we rapped off safely. No big deal.

Gordon knew I was in the Tetons with Mike and came up on a whim to join us. He gladly took over as Mike's partner for more Teton routes, while I amused myself on the boulders around Jenny Lake and Blacktail Butte, a small limestone outcrop few Teton climbers bothered with. Mike thought me bonkers, but I was happy to be doing something more technical and finger intensive versus yet another mind-numbing alpine hike. The boulders at Jenny Lake had been the playground of the bouldering visionary John Gill, who, in the 1950s and 1960s, contrived difficult, dynamic lines up their overhanging faces, applying his notorious strength to do moves that were far ahead of their time. I was curious to see how I'd measure up to some of Gill's problems. The answer was: not especially well, but I was able to entertain myself for hours on these "mini classics."

Gordon had to leave after a few days, and I was not down for hanging out in the Tetons anymore and said so to Mike. He was in a good mood after getting some desired climbs under his belt, so he acquiesced; we'd go to the rock-climbing paradise of Boulder, Colorado, at least for a little while. He rationalized it would be good to work on his rock skills. I had a slew of routes I couldn't wait to do, all harvested from the pages of *CLIMB!,* a book published the previous year. *CLIMB!* was all about Colorado rock climbing, and especially highlighted the Boulder area. Beyond its gripping stories of first ascents and the progression of difficulty, the book's dramatic black-and-white photos of climbers clinging to impossibly steep walls made my hands clammy with a nervous sweat.

When we drove into Eldorado Canyon State Park a day later, my pulse kicked up a few notches. My eyes landed on the long, regal buttress of Redgarden Wall, with the arête of a famous 5.11 route, the *Naked Edge,* jutting hundreds of feet into the cobalt sky. The constant roar of the river coursing through the canyon added wildness to the atmosphere. The morning air chilled my skin, adding more goosebumps to the ones already there from anticipation.

We started with some easier rock climbs, and what I found calmed me. The rock was different from my beloved Shawangunk cliffs, of course, with the Eldorado rock being dark-red sandstone, but still trustworthy and solid. The climbs tended to have short cruxes followed by rests on bigger holds and easier climbing—a lot like the Gunks. And the protection was usually good, at least by the standards I was used to at home. Meanwhile, my confidence soared as I realized that most of the *CLIMB!* photos had been taken with a wide-angle lens, making the routes look a lot bigger and scarier than they actually were.

A longtime local climber, Jim Erickson, would soon publish a guide to the canyon employing a new, very nifty rating system for protection based on the Motion Picture Association of America's rating system for movies. On Erickson's scale, "G" meant great gear placements were available and close to the hardest moves. "PG" meant the gear was adequate, but not necessarily nearby while executing the cruxes. On a PG route, the leader might be in for a longer but not necessarily life-threatening fall if he blew it. "R" meant you had better be solid at the grade—the gear was good enough to keep you alive, but a fall could easily result in a broken limb or an extended stay at the hospital. And "X" meant you were essentially free soloing—a lead fall on an X route meant death, or failing that, probably wishing you had died rather than suffer the permanent injuries you'd surely experience. Having a clue about what to expect protection-wise became a game-changer, allowing us to not need "insider" info on how dangerous (or not) a climb was.

Mike and I stayed with friends from UVM who'd rented a house for the summer. The extra company was good. Mike was able to climb with someone happy to join him in nearby Rocky Mountain National Park for a long alpine route, while I teamed up with whoever was free to climb at Eldorado or on the local granite crags of Boulder Canyon. Occasionally, Mike and I climbed easier routes in Eldorado, but he found the climbing difficult and didn't really like it. I wanted to do at least one longer alpine climb with Mike and to see Rocky Mountain National Park. We spent a day on a fun, multi-pitch 5.8 on the Petit Grepon, a small rock tower with a spectacular summit. The summer alpine terrain of tundra, tarns, and high, craggy peaks provided postcard views in all directions, and I enjoyed it—even the five-mile approach hike.

Late one afternoon, I returned to the house from a good day of climbing to find the place buzzing with activity. Camping and climbing gear were scattered on the living room floor, as the boys stuffed it all into backpacks. The whole gang, including Mike, had impulsively decided to go up to the Wind Rivers. They were leaving in a couple hours, and I had a decision to make: join them or stay in Boulder at the soon-to-be-empty house. I had zero interest in going to the Winds. I was climbing well, getting stronger, and having a blast on rock. Still, once my friends were gone, the big house was going to be lonely, and it would be tough to scrounge up weekday climbing partners. So, I filled the gas tank and started driving west on I-70 into the evening.

The colorful sunset buoyed my spirit, the sky over the Colorado Plateau turning deep blue then pitch black, lit only by a speckling of stars. Later, I spotted the glow of Las Vegas on the horizon long before the casinos' gaudy neon jumped above the skyline. I drove through the night, playing the radio loudly and singing along to cassette tapes by Led Zeppelin, the Rolling Stones, and Supertramp to stay awake. When I started to nod off, I plucked my toothbrush from my toilet kit and brushed away for a long spell. You'll never fall asleep at the wheel while brushing your teeth. I crossed into California as the desert dawned, toward the Los Angeles Basin and merging on to I-5 southbound. I had butterflies in my stomach along with a gnawing doubt: was this a good gambit or not?

During my junior year at UVM, I'd lived in a communal arrangement on campus in a special dorm comprised of co-ed suites. The idea behind the living quarters was for students with similar passions to share their experiences and grow together through them. Our program, "Wilderness Sports," consisted of a dozen students involved in outdoor activities from hiking to kayaking to, of course, climbing. When the semester began, I became infatuated with one young lady in our program, until I'd eventually fallen totally in love with her.

Melinda Rutledge was a petite woman with amazing bright-blue eyes and short dark hair. She had an easy laugh and way about her that attracted me in a fashion I'd never felt before, but my advances yielded only a close friendship right up until the end of the school year. At that point, we dated briefly, only to have it crash and burn. The end had come abruptly, and I didn't understand why Melinda had had second thoughts about our relationship. All I knew is that I was crushed.

I'd called her several times during my trip out west, hoping that maybe, just maybe, she was open to trying again. Those conversations were friendly and lengthy, but we avoided anything directly confronting our previous intimacy, instead parrying around the edges of a topic that, for me, was still a fragile scab. Melinda was living in Southern California that summer, and when the Boulder gang headed to the Wind Rivers, I decided to visit her. However, Melinda didn't know I was on my way. All I had was her address and a heart full of hope.

When I got to Encinitas, I washed up at a gas station and drove to Melinda's place. My hand trembled as I rang the doorbell. Doubt clouded my mind. She had to be home at this early hour, but what if someone else came to the door? What would I say? I'd just driven a thousand miles; I was over-caffeinated, sleep deprived, and dressed in grubby climbing garb I'd worn too many consecutive days without laundering.

Melinda opened the door, shocked to see me. Then she stepped back for a moment, her hand covering her mouth. Was she about to scream? Her face took a moment to turn from surprise into mirth, and those bright-blue eyes said all I needed to know. A wave of relief rolled through my body when she grabbed me by the waist and enveloped me in a big hug. I returned the gesture, hugging her tightly and taking my first breath since arriving at her doorstep. Melinda led me straight to the shower and gave me a clean towel. After I scrubbed up, she took me by the hand to her bed.

My timing had been perfect. Melinda had a free week before meeting friends in the Bay Area, so we packed up her belongings and pointed the truck toward Yosemite. With us seated hip-to-hip on the bench seat of the truck, we crept out of the Southern California coastal gridlock into the open space of the Sierra's East Side, her hand cradled in mine. We stopped in Lone Pine for the night, cooking dinner on my stove in a little park, and then slept in the back of the truck. We hiked in the mountains for a day and wandered around the moonscape of Mono Lake before chugging up the long grade of Tioga Pass into Yosemite National Park. When we hit the entrance, I realized I was completely ignorant of the local geography. I knew about the Valley, of course, home to iconic monoliths like Half Dome and El Capitan, but knew nothing of the high country of Tuolumne Meadows, beyond the pass. In fact, I'd never even heard of the place. We drove slowly to take in the green meadows interspersed with groves of giant pines marching up to huge walls of rock. Each bend in the road revealed a scene more stunning than the last. The granite domes just screamed climbing. I felt like I'd entered heaven.

We stopped at the small seasonal general store for a snack and to get better oriented when serendipity happened yet again.

There, we ran into two friends from the Gunks, Paul and Iza Trapani. They had a campsite on Tenaya Lake and convinced us to terminate our plan to go to the Valley and stay with them instead. Paul explained the Valley, thousands of feet lower in elevation than Tuolumne, would be hot, crowded, and unpleasant, while here, at nine thousand feet, the climbing conditions would be perfect, and the mountain air fresh. Melinda and I were easily convinced. We spent a week climbing amazing routes on the knob-studded granite, sharing campfire meals with our friends, and rekindling our relationship. At the end of those idyllic seven days, I dropped her off in a town near the park, then pointed the truck east toward Boulder. I was sad leaving her, but as I did, I had a smile on my face—I knew we had a future together.

Back in Boulder, the gang had just returned from a successful trip to the Wind Rivers. The room was full of laughter and the stink of unwashed climber bodies, fresh out of the mountains. Mike was happy, still riding the high from his trip, but he was not enthusiastic about being back in Boulder and made that crystal clear. He said he was going to return east, with or without me. He'd fly back if I didn't agree to leave. I wanted to stay another week or two and climb, figuring my savings would last about that long. But without Mike to split the gas money, I was not going to be able to afford staying in Boulder and driving home.

We made an abrupt departure the next morning and endured an uncomfortable drive back east. Cassette-deck tunes filled the truck, a space otherwise devoid of words. The only thoughts we verbalized along the nearly two thousand miles concerned our most basic human and travel needs: "I need to piss," "I'm hungry," and "We need gas." I silently wished we had a third person along to lessen the awkwardness. Neither Mike nor I were in the mood to delve into the reasons for the gulf between us. I knew I hadn't lived up to the bargain we'd made for our trip, but I was pissed I had to leave Colorado earlier than I wanted. The summer's trip solidified and defined my true passion. When I'd started climbing just two short years before, I was certain I'd be heading for mountains and remote ranges. Now, however, I knew I didn't give a shit about summiting peaks. I was committed to rock climbing and trying my damndest to be good at it. For Mike and me, that didn't leave a lot of space for compromise. Resentment was our common ground.

We didn't stop driving until we got to my parents' house late on a muggy summer night, quietly rolling our sleeping bags out on the back lawn to get some shuteye. I slept soundly for a few hours before my mother woke us in the morning, surprised but happy to see us there.

I drove Mike to a bus station so he could finish his journey home, sending him off with a terse goodbye. After a long drive saying nothing to each other, it wasn't time to start exploring our shared disappointments in each other. Mike and I didn't speak again for months.

I returned to Vermont for my last year of college, psyched as ever on rock climbing and in love with a woman I had chased for the better part of a year. The time Melinda and I spent in Tuolumne formed a bond, a chemistry between us somehow never created by the previous year living in proximity on campus. Maybe Tuolumne was a magic land after all.

I knew I loved Melinda, and I also knew I needed to return

to the Valley to climb. Tuolumne was gorgeous and enchanting, but one of the most intriguing views was to the west where Half Dome rises up like an overlord, with one eye on the high country and another on the void below. Endless walls of granite stretched on both sides of that deep chasm. I had to explore those walls—to see them from below and climb them.

My UVM buddy Gordon agreed to join me on a trip to Yosemite once school ended, with our main objective being to climb *The Nose* route on El Capitan, Yosemite's biggest wall, standing 3,000 feet above the valley floor. Immediately after graduation, we hit the road. We rolled into the Valley on a cool mid-May morning, the air so clear we could easily pick out teams of climbers on the wall and get a better sense of the scale of the monolith. I found myself just a little disappointed, seeing those specks of humans scattered around the cliff. My mind had built up El Cap as this gigantic, unfathomable thing, so huge as to be almost impossible. But now I could piece together the lines just by looking at the climbers following them. El Cap was doable for us. I didn't say anything aloud, but I do remember thinking, "It's not *that* big."

We got a tent site in Camp 4, the traditional climbers' campground. The scene was a mélange of climbers from around the world plus the locals, who kept permanent residence at a couple sites. The visiting climbers were friendly, but most of the local hoi polloi were standoffish. When I passed by their camp sites, I felt like an interloper crashing a party. It was a look I'd get—a quick stare without a greeting, if they noted me at all. I was definitely not part of the "in" crew, and I felt it. But that was okay; I wanted to keep a low profile, especially since I was a first timer in the Valley. Camp 4 was more intimidating than the giant walls surrounding us, especially when I watched some of the resident talents pull off impossible-looking boulder problems on the smooth granite blocks scattered about the campground.

We started off with easy routes. Gordon was more accustomed to granite cracks than me, having started climbing on similar rock near his home in Colorado. Still, I got the hang of it quickly, even if the climbing style was so different from the Gunks, where what lay ahead was often a mystery, hidden over the lip of an overhang. Here, the crack lines didn't hold many secrets—singling out the harder bits was often just a matter of seeing where the climb was steepest.

One route on our "must-do" list was *The Good Book/Right Side of the Folly*, a popular five-pitch 5.10+. We got there early, hoping to beat any potential competition, but we found one party already several pitches up. They were obviously competent and moving well, so they wouldn't be an issue for us. I took the first, 5.9 pitch and belayed Gordon up. Gordon styled the next pitch, grunting only minimally on the crux bulge, and then called down that I was on belay. I climbed through the crux smoothly and was laybacking on easier terrain when the world suddenly began to shake. I held on and looked up toward Gordon. A couple of Stoppers fell out of the crack, rattling down the rope to me. I shuffled upward at a manic, adrenaline-fueled pace while the world continued to vibrate, reaching Gordon at his stance just as the earthquake subsided. The quake, as sudden and frightening as it had been, showed an advantage to the new "Friends"—a recently invented type of protection for cracks. Friends have four spring-loaded lobes that hold the device in place inside a parallel-sided fissure. Because of these springs, the Friends had expanded and contracted with the crack as the pillar wobbled, staying put where Gordon had seated them, while many of the nuts he'd placed on his lead had fallen out.

We pondered what to do next: continue up or bail off. Would there be aftershocks? Figuring the worst was over, we decided to continue. As I readied the rack to lead the next pitch, the party ahead of us rappelled to our belay station. They had been on top of the pillar, which stands 700 feet tall, when the quake hit, and said the damn thing was wobbling so hard they thought it was going to break off and take them with it. We changed our minds and rapped off behind them.

Back in Camp 4, we ran into a friend of mine from the Gunks, Greg. While we caught up and talked plans, Greg said he'd love to join us on *The Nose*, so Gordon and I had a brief discussion and figured there could be safety in numbers; it was the first big wall for all of us, with three thousand feet and thirty-some pitches of steep granite. The route, while not considered too difficult by the standards of 1980, was still an undertaking for experienced climbers—which, when it came to El Capitan, we decidedly were not.

Gordon and Greg climbed four pitches on the first day, aid climbing to Sickle Ledge. I spent the day doing last-minute errands and registering our intent to climb *The Nose* with the National Park Service. Gordon and Greg rappelled back to the ground late in the afternoon, leaving our ropes anchored in place—fixed—for us to ascend the next day using mechanical rope ascenders called Jumars. We packed our food, water, and bivy gear into two huge haulbags, each the size of a large army duffle bag and weighing over fifty pounds.

In the morning, I dropped Greg and Gordon off at the short trail to the base of El Cap with our haulbags and drove back to Camp 4 to park my truck. Hitching a ride back to El Cap, I got picked up by Ray Jardine, a famous Yosemite climber and the inventor of Friends. Ray gave me a bunch of last-minute tips when I explained it was our first big wall. He'd spent a lot of time on *The Nose* trying to free-climb the route in its entirety. He knew every inch of the climb from his attempts, including having almost climbed it in a single day in 1974 with two partners. The trio barely missed the twenty-four-hour mark after being pinned by a storm—an amazing feat for the era. The route would finally be done in one day the next year, by Jim Bridwell, John Long, and Billy Westbay, to much fanfare.

I sprinted up the trail to the route and stared up at the cliff, getting my first real up-close gander at where we planned to climb. Gordon and Greg had already started Jumaring the fixed lines up to our high point. They looked tiny against the thousands of feet of gray and gold granite above them, while the last half of El Capitan—the bulging headwalls that loomed above the lower apron—looked ridiculously steep from below. I stopped looking up and got my own gear together. Gordon and Greg got to the first anchor and began the arduous procedure of hauling the two bags up, using their Jumars and slings to foot-haul and capture the bags' progress in a technique that had been invented years earlier in the Valley by the big-wall pioneer Royal Robbins. Gordon and I had practiced the hauling technique on a cliff in New Hampshire earlier in the spring, figuring out the system. It worked fine then, with a small bag with perhaps thirty-fivec pounds of crap in it. But now, the bags' 100 pounds of combined weight with all the food and water for the three of us meant they hardly budged off the ground. I gave them a push from underneath, and they started to inch up at a glacial pace. A couple of climbers walking by stopped to look up at us. "How long you planning on being up there? A month?" one yelled. I felt foolish and said nothing.

We cursed and sweated our way up to Sickle Ledge,

blaspheming those lumbering bags every time they hung up on some small protrusion. We eventually got ourselves and our luggage four pitches up the route, with another daunting thirty or so to go. The work for the day was done, but we'd barely started. My first impression of El Cap not being all that big had been wrong. Getting ourselves and those two fat bags up what was clearly a monstrous piece of stone had revealed itself to be a Herculean task. Any arrogance I'd started the day with had dissolved like a morning mist.

Sickle Ledge did not afford much space for a cozy snooze. Greg and Gordon settled into cramped positions for the night, tucked in fetal positions. I opted to use a small hammock I had purchased for this climb. The thing was simply a nylon sheet with a couple straps on the sides that came to a single tie-in point in the middle to clip into the anchor. Meanwhile, a plastic spreader bar slipped between the straps to keep an opening around the head and shoulders. When I first got into the hammock and slid in the spreader bar, it felt pretty comfortable—a little snug, but surely better than what my friends were enduring. I woke a couple hours later, my shoulders aching and my back stiff. I needed to shift my body, but I couldn't easily move in the hammock—it felt like fighting a giant python. At one point, as I struggled to shift onto my side, I accidently knocked out the spreader bar. I listened to it "tink, tink, tink" down the cliff for five hundred feet before finding its final resting place in the talus. Now I was beyond uncomfortable: my face was enveloped in this torture sack, and I could barely breathe. All I could do was count the minutes until sunrise.

I wasn't the only one who'd slept poorly, and there was little morning banter. As we finished our breakfasts in silence, Greg suddenly announced he no longer wanted any part of this adventure. He'd had an epiphany during the night, and didn't see much upside to pushing two big, fat haulbags up three thousand feet of rock. It was understandable. We weren't exactly crushing it—a trio of banana slugs could have beaten us to the top. Gordon and I didn't try to talk him out of it, and it wouldn't have done any good anyway: Greg was going down. We didn't realize it then, but his departure was our saving grace. When we reassessed our needs and repacked, we eliminated an entire haulbag and all that surplus weight. Greg rapped off with the extra bag while Gordon and I prepared to continue upward. Getting rid of the extra gear lightened our mood as well as our load.

Gordon led a pitch that traversed right a good distance, to the base of the Stove Legs crack system, a wide crack so named for the sawed-off woodstove legs that had been used as ersatz pitons to protect it on the first ascent, back in the late 1950s. When he called for the haulbag, I detached it from the anchor and let it swing out. The bag was moving fast when it crashed into the corner system below Gordon, but it didn't split open, and I breathed a sigh of relief.

A couple pitches later, while cleaning a pitch Gordon had led, I felt water dripping on me from above. I looked up to his anchor and saw that the haulbag had formed a small wet spot on the bottom. I mentioned it to Gordon, and we decided we would deal with it when we stopped for the night on El Cap Tower, about one thousand feet up the wall. We arrived there in the late afternoon, tired but content. We were moving much better as a party of two and especially with just the one haulbag. In fact, you might even say we were having fun. We had a large flat space to sleep on, and a fine view of the valley floor below our feet. But when we opened our haulbag, our smiles evaporated. Every single water bottle had exploded when the bag hit the corner, and our gear inside was soaked. We had exactly zero water, our sleeping bags were wet, and we were thirsty. We'd not taken a big water break during the day, having only sipped from the one, now-empty water bottle we kept outside the bag at belays. Rummaging around the ledge, we were lucky to find a few plastic bottles of water another party had cached. We figured this was a sign, a signal to press on. We drank up, ate dinner, and slept like the dead on our blessedly large, flat ledge.

The next morning the euphoria of finding the stashed water had faded and we needed to reckon with reality. We still had about half the water we'd found, a little less than a gallon, but it likely wouldn't be enough to get us to the top, some 2,000 feet higher. Were the gods with us? Should we rap? Take our chances? It was another gorgeous, early-June day in Yosemite. The morning light bathed El Cap Meadow a thousand feet below us but hadn't yet reached us on the wall. The slight chill in the shadowed air refreshed us. We decided to gamble, betting that we'd find more stashed water on this popular climb.

We breezed up the landmarks of Texas and Boot flakes, both thin features seemingly pasted to the wall, and then ascended to the Gray Ledges, now about two thousand feet up our route, drinking our remaining water along the way. Our camp on the ledges, which admittedly were not as deluxe as El Cap Tower, was below the Great Roof, an imposing overhang a couple hundred feet above us. We found more water on the Gray Ledges—not as much as the night before, but enough to get us through dinner and keep us hydrated.

We started the following morning with only a few swigs of water left, but now confident of our ability to get to the top of El Cap. We slowly climbed the steep crack system in our aiders;

like the proverbial tortoise, we were in a good groove. We spent our final night at Camp 6, about four hundred feet from the top. It was a slightly uneven ledge with a wide crack in the back. The scent emanating from the dark crevice told the story of its use as a latrine during bivouacs past.

We were parched, and we'd failed to find any more cached water bottles along the way. But Gordon had a plan. He peered down that dank shithole of a crack and, after a moment of silent consideration, reached in. Gordon fished around the putrid crevice, stretching until his armpit stopped further extension. Then he grinned as he pulled up a large plastic bottle half filled with something we both hoped was water.

"Dude," I said, "I dunno, man . . ." The bottle was covered in duct tape, and impossible to see into.

Gordon reached in again, garnering a second bottle, also partially filled and covered in tape. We were suspicious, but desperate for a drink. Gordon uncapped the first bottle and took a sniff before handing it to me.

"Waddaaya think?" he asked.

I sniffed and it smelt like water, maybe stale and too long in a plastic bottle, but probably water. I still hesitated because of its origin. That crack was fucking gross, but we were also fucking thirsty. We carefully sampled the liquid, each taking a small sip at first. It was water, and it tasted sweet. Sips turned to gulps.

The stench aside, the Camp 6 ledge was a cool spot. The trees in the Valley now looked like tiny toothpicks under our feet; the cars winding along the road were toys. We were higher than anything else around us, save the top of El Cap itself, and we'd be there a few hours after waking the next morning.

I thought about Ray Jardine trying to free *The Nose*. It seemed like a ridiculous quest to me. We had spent most of our time in slings, aiding our way up the route, and parts of it looked flat-out impossible to free-climb. To my eyes, many of the cracks were too thin to jam fingers, some of the faces between the cracks looked impossibly blank, and the dihedral walls high on the route were too smooth and glassy. I thought if he or anyone succeeded, it would certainly be the most impressive feat of climbing, ever. Ray kept trying, but it didn't happen for him.

Thirteen years later, in 1993, *The Nose* would finally be freed. It was not only an impressive show of climbing skill, but one of the most impressive athletic feats ever—and quite possibly the single most significant athletic feat of the twentieth century. While many highly talented climbers spent countless months and years trying to free *The Nose*, it wasn't a Camp 4 denizen who did it, but rather a petite, five-foot-tall woman who I hadn't even heard of back in 1980 named Lynn Hill.

BON VOYAGE! WHAT'S UP ACROSS THE SEA?

"Because in the end, you won't remember the times you spent in the office or mowing your lawn. Climb that goddam mountain!"

—Jack Kerouac

In the 1970s and through the 1980s, the Gunks were a "must visit" place for any serious climber looking to do some of the hardest rock climbs in the world. Several visitors in the fall of 1980 were especially impressive. Alex Lowe was one of them—he was a fountain of energy, a perpetual-motion machine. Fueled by an endless appetite for strong coffee and climbing, he would get up earlier than anyone else just to knock out hundreds of pull-ups before breakfast. Alex was tall and lanky, with a thatch of brown hair topping his smiling face. He had a habit of rotating through partners as he wore them out, one by one, climbing well past twilight. Alex was an excellent rock climber, even though his heart and larger ambitions lived in the mountains. His skinny legs and rail-thin body belied his ability to trot uphill all day. He was described in the mountaineering world as "the lung with two legs."

Other visitors that fall included the Australians Kim Carrigan and Louise Shepherd. Kim was one of the strongest climbers of the era, and Louise among the finest female rock climbers. Kim was all sinew, tendon, and rippling muscle, wrapped in a tight sheath of skin. If there was any fat on him, it was hidden deep beneath the surface. His brash nature turned off a lot of people, especially in America. Kim happily told you what he did, how quickly he did it, and how easy it had been for him. He even managed to tweak the always-jovial "Mayor," Kevin Bein, after Kim told him he'd done the 5.12 roof *Kansas City*. Kevin opined, "Oh, that's such a beautiful route!" and Kim's response was a dismissive, "It's not really very hard." Kevin retorted, "I didn't say it was hard. I said it was beautiful!" None of Carrigan's bravado bothered me—he backed his talk with action, ripping through hard routes in minimal tries. In any event, Louise, Kim's girlfriend and principal climbing partner, had a way of taking Kim down a notch with a quip if he got too full of himself.

Melinda still had a year of school left, and I planned to stay in Burlington while she completed her studies. She found us a little apartment, and I took a job at the nearby outdoor shop, Eastern Mountain Sports, working in the warehouse. When the weekends arrived, I drove to the Gunks with Melinda, climbing with Carrigan and Alex as much as I could. Those guys could hold on to small edges forever while figuring out sequences under pressure, well above their last protection. I was endlessly inspired by their willpower to keep fighting through hard moves. Carrigan was an especially well-traveled rock climber. He told me about all the different places he'd visited—England, West Germany, and France among them—fueling my already formidable wanderlust. Kim also knew that I wanted to get better at rock climbing.

"If you really want to be a great climber, Russ, you've got to travel. It's the only way you'll learn and test yourself," he told me one day. "You've got to climb with as many great climbers as you can, and climb on as many different types of rock as possible. It's how you'll reach your potential."

By the time of Kim's visit, I'd climbed a bunch of 5.11s at various areas around the country, but I'd not broken into the 5.12 grade, where climbing royalty dwelled. There were not a lot of 5.12s anywhere in 1980, and 5.13s were almost mythical. Only three existed in the country—maybe the world—Tony Yaniro's *Grand Illusion* near Lake Tahoe, California, Ray Jardine's *Phoenix* in Yosemite, and the very recent *Cosmic Debris* by Bill Price, also in Yosemite Valley. There were no 5.13s at all back East.

I knew I had to climb a 5.12. I needed to feel what it took.

While I had a selection of 5.12s to choose from in the Gunks, only a few offered excellent protection. *Supercrack*, which had seen only four or five ascents in the six years since Steve Wunsch first climbed it, was one. Even though its briefly suggested grade of 5.13 didn't stand after a couple Californians with superior crack-climbing ability repeated it, *Supercrack* was still thought to be a "hard" 5.12. *Gravity's Rainbow*, a John Bragg creation at Lost City, was supposed to be very difficult, also at the high end of the 5.12 spectrum. I figured those two were outside the realm of possibility for me. *Kansas City*, a twenty-foot roof with a crack running its length, was the last option for safe falls.

Kansas City had, by far, the most ascents and was thought to be an "easy" 5.12, an oxymoron of that era if ever there was one. But it had a lot going for it besides being an "easy" 5.12, including a quick approach from the road and a short section of simple 5.4 climbing to get to a comfortable stance at the base of the roof. John Bragg knocked out the first free ascent during the era-defining year of 1973, and the route was an absolute classic, requiring powerful, gymnastic moves on the underbelly of that big overhang.

My buddy Doug Strickholm and I checked out *Kansas City* a couple times that fall, usually at the end of our climbing day and putting in only half-hearted attempts. We never got very far, falling quickly after the first couple of moves. Abiding by the yo-yo style of the time, we returned to the belay stance at the base of the roof after each fall. Carrigan knew I'd been trying the climb and encouraged me to keep at it. I decided to get serious, stop screwing around with half-assed sessions, and start training hard in preparation.

Before the advent of plastic holds, hangboards, or climbing gyms, training meant lifting free weights in our Burlington apartment and doing a regimen of "hangs" and pull-ups while at work in the EMS warehouse. There, I'd hung a simple but effective training device—comprised of a length of four-inch-diameter pipe—across an aisle, affixing it to the shelving with slings. The pipe rolled in the slings, making me constantly adjust my grip. I would knock out ten pull-ups then hang on the bar until I couldn't anymore, my forearms swollen with lactic acid. After a short rest, I'd repeat the process, increasing the number of pull-ups and hanging from that blasted pipe until my arms screamed. My backroom regimen became a daily workout: move boxes onto shelves, do a series of pull-ups and hangs for ten minutes, move more boxes, repeat. By the end of the day, I'd knocked out hundreds of pull-ups and dozens of hangs, with the shop manager no more the wiser. My forearms became Popeye-like after a month, and my endurance increased exponentially.

Doug and I had discovered during our earliest attempts on *Kansas City's* big roof that going barefoot was a better solution than trying it in the clunky, stiff footwear of the era, which made it hard to grip the smaller holds. With our naked toes, we could grab holds like chimpanzees, never losing our lower body's connection to the roof and avoiding swinging off the miserly handholds. On a cold November day, we soloed up the short bit of 5.4 rock to the stance and set up the belay. Doug and I gave the roof a couple tries, with the same result as past attempts—coming up short on a long reach off an awkward finger jam to a big, sloping hold. But something was different that day. I felt stronger—a lot stronger—and the holds felt bigger. I knew I could do this thing.

I tied in and took my socks off. Chalking up my feet in preparation, I double-checked my knot and grabbed the big opening hold. I slithered out the first moves and slotted my fingers into the awkward jam, but then made a bigger twisting motion with my hips than I had previously. That movement brought my body closer to the rock, my hips parallel with the plane of the ceiling instead of sagging toward the ground. It was just enough of a change, and I snagged that large, sloping hold for my first time.

There was no way I was letting go. I got a good hand jam in the crack, tucked a naked foot as deeply as I could, and placed a nut. Out near the lip of the giant overhang, I stopped to clip an old fixed piton; my body felt like it was levitating, like I was glued to the roof. *All my training had paid off!* I grabbed a huge spike at the lip of the roof and matched hands, cutting my feet loose then maneuvering my thigh onto the spike to clear the overhang. As soon as I stood on that spike, I was at the top of the cliff. I let out a whoop of success as Doug hooted, "Welcome to the 5.12 club!"

Melinda and I planned a climbing trip to Europe for the summer of 1981, with our first stop in Britain. The Brits had more established rock climbing than any other European country—at least as far as climbs done in the free-climbing style that conformed to traditional American rules and ethics. Before we left on our voyage, we still made our weekend trips to the Gunks, and that's when I met the visiting British climber Pete O'Donovan.

Brits regularly made pilgrimages to the Gunks in the early- and mid-1980s, and most of the time I knew their names and reputations, but I had never heard of Pete. He was tall and skinny, with toothpick legs but strong-looking arms. He came solo and was teaming up with whoever would go climb with him. I was happy to do so, especially since I could glean info for our upcoming journey. Out on the rock, it didn't take long to see he was good—really good. When he casually talked about famous routes he'd done back in Britain, I wondered why I'd not heard of him before. Despite his low-profile, his résumé included some of the hardest routes in the British climbing epicenter of the Peak District, climbs like *London Wall* (5.11+), *White Wall* (5.12), and *Profit of Doom* (5.12-) for starters—famous gritstone routes I'd heard of and hoped to do myself. Pete's talent was evident as soon as I watched him grab the stone. Even under the duress of some of the Gunks' most dangerous climbs—climbs like Sky Top's *Cries and Whimpers* (5.11 R/X) and the super-testy *To Have or Have Not* (5.12 R), on which a fall in the wrong place could send you to the hospital—he still moved solidly and fluidly. I belayed him as he almost flashed *Supercrack*, falling on the very last move before the end of the difficulties. I couldn't believe it; I had to pick my jaw off the ground as I watched him almost top it out on his first go. Kim Carrigan had managed the first one-day ascent of the route, a huge deal, just months before. Now Pete showed an even higher bar of performance. O'Donovan hiked the route on his second go, and while watching him, I got a new perspective on what was possible. Pete was the best rock climber I'd ever seen, much less ever partnered with, and he gave me an idea of the level of talent I could expect to witness in England.

Melinda and I arrived in London on a sunny morning in early June. We collected our two backpacks, which had the gear we'd need for our three-month trip: tent, sleeping bags and pads, cooking stove plus basic utensils. I wore my only decent pair of slacks on the flight. My other pair of climbing pants was packed with the rest of the climbing wardrobe: a few T-shirts, a sweater, spare socks, a raincoat, and a pair of shorts. My carry-on bag was my small climbing pack and had all of my essentials: climbing shoes, rack, and harness.

Our first stop was a visit to Tideford to see our friend Strappo and his girlfriend, Pud. They'd lived in the Peak District for years but had recently moved to Southwest England for Pud to pursue a degree in linguistics. Strappo's employment prospects there were less than stellar, so he worked picking potatoes for indentured-servant wages before shifting to being a ticket collector on a double-decker bus.

I'd met the couple the previous year in Yosemite, which morphed into giving them a ride to Boulder afterward and doing a bunch of climbing with Strappo. Strappo's nickname was a shortening of *strapombiombo,* Italian for "overhang," which was used to describe his less-than-athletic belly, kept round by his thirst for beer. Despite the extra luggage around his waist, Strappo was a good climber, with a quick wit and easygoing manner. Amusingly, he was the architect of many impish antics, and his hilarious stories kept me laughing for hours. I'd never heard of the "Hammerhead Shark," "One-Eyed Trouser Snake," or "Joan of Arc," all various tricks performed with one's dick and requiring simple props: a matchstick, a glass eye, and lighter fluid. Strappo was happy to describe these in detail, and with enough beer in him, demonstrate on occasion. The reason for Pud's moniker, unfortunately, is lost to my memory. I'm not sure how it went down in Britain, but her nickname got quite a few chuckles when they were in the States.

Strappo introduced me to British rock in a horrifying fashion. On the shores of North Devon's Culm Coast lie large, steep, damp cliffs of shale, a soft, crumbly rock that most sane climbers avoid. Our destination was a dark-gray crag called Blackchurch, and the day started off cloudy, making the flat sea look like an oil slick and the scary cliff look even gloomier. Ripples of water came down in small streams along its length, and even the dry parts looked as slick as a parquet floor. As we walked along the cobbled beach at the cliff base, Strappo picked out a route for us to start our day.

"Ooooh, yes, we MUST do this one!" he chirped. "It's the perfect introduction to Blackchurch: pretty well protected for this type of rock and only E1 5c—and it looks pretty dry as well."

I looked up at the wall. The climb took a steep corner system with obvious wet patches here and there. *E1 5c—hmmm.* I vaguely understood the grading system. British grading harkens back to much simpler days in the evolution of rock climbing, and the adjectives sound accordingly quaint and antiquated. They start off simply enough: "Easy" is the term for, well, the easy routes. Next is "Moderate," a step up. From there, we go to "Difficult," then "Hard Difficult, "Very Difficult," and "Hard Very Difficult." At this point, the old timers ran out of modifiers for "difficult," so they moved on to "Severe," "Hard Severe," and "Hard Very Severe."

The last entry, saved for the very hardest climbs, is "Extremely Severe"—or simply "Extreme." As the years passed and evermore-testy routes got done, the E grades split numerically into E1, E2, etc.

The grading system doesn't stop with the adjectives, however; there's also the "technical" grade to consider. This grade telegraphs how difficult a climb's hardest moves are, using numbers followed by a, b, or c—as in 3a, 3b, 3c, and so forth. When mixing the adjective with the technical grade, a bit of alchemy is involved. If there's a high adjective followed by a low technical grade, say, E4 5a, the route is probably very sustained in nature with few rests, poorly protected, or on suspect rock. Possibly all the above. A high technical grade with a lower adjective, like E1 6b, probably means a short, difficult crux, excellent protection, or both. In any case, the system potentially provided a lot more information than the Yosemite Decimal System used in the States, but until one samples a bunch of climbs and figures it out, it's just confusing. Now, staring at the climb above me, all "E1 5c" meant was: frightening, difficult, and I could possibly take a bad fall; at the very least, I'd get wet, with water dripping down my forearms.

Once I tied in and started climbing, I was pleasantly surprised. The rock had many small, positive holds that remained invisible until they were at eye level, and the protection was okay. Then, out of nowhere, a loud crash echoed along the cliff. A huge hunk of rock had fallen off, for no apparent reason, about a hundred yards from us. I stopped climbing, standing on small holds and doubting the wisdom of continuing. Was this climb about to suffer a similar fate? I looked down at Strappo, fifty feet below me.

"Oh, don't mind that," he said. "*That* section of cliff down there is crap, and we won't go near it." I climbed on, albeit a lot less relaxed than I'd been before the cliff decomposed.

When the tide went out, we hopped across seaweed-slick cobbles to a seastack, a seventy-foot spire that looked like a gigantic piece of pie tilted onto its wide, outer edge, with its point rising to the sky. There were big holes through the side of it, slots that gave open views along the shoreline and evidence of the constant erosive effects of the ocean. On the face looking out on the Atlantic was a beautiful thin crack splitting the smooth shale, top to bottom. *Sacre Coeur* was certainly the classic pitch of the area, with positive jams, plenty of protection, and solid rock—well, solid for Blackchurch. I slotted my fingers securely into the crack's constrictions, hardly able to contain an ear-to-ear grin as I climbed. That route changed my mind about Blackchurch, though I never did return. Back at his home, I asked Strappo if we might visit a better cliff, one less predisposed to eroding in front of our noses.

"Bosigran!" Strappo exclaimed. "That's where we've got to go. Ooh yes, brilliant climbing, gorgeous ocean, solid granite—can't beat it!"

"Great, Strappo, let's hit it," I said.

But then a look of concern crossed his face as he muttered, "Ummm, yeah, we should do. We must figure how to get there." We'd ridden with friends in their car for our day at Blackchurch, and it hadn't dawned on me to ponder the condition of Strappo's wheels.

"Can't we use your car?" My stomach sank as I asked, knowing the answer was going to be problematic.

"Unfortunately," Strappo began, "Belsen—that's my car's

name—is knackered, defunct, shuffled off this mortal coil, pushin' up the daisies. It's not working."

It turned out that Strappo's rig did, in fact, work, but Belsen had issues. On a recent drive, he'd been pulled over and fined for emitting too much exhaust and noise. I asked him to start the car. The engine turned over immediately, but even at idle, the car was thunderous and spewed copious white smoke. We quickly traced the issue to a big hole in the exhaust pipe.

"Strappo, let's say Belsen didn't belch smoke or hit rock-concert decibels—do you think it would be okay to drive?" I asked.

"Suppose so," he answered, "but I'm flat broke. Can't afford to fix it."

I rummaged in his garage and found a tin can. We cut the can and wrapped it around the exhaust pipe, affixing it as tightly as we could with two hose clamps and clothes-hanger wire. This time when we started the car, it sounded tons better, with very little smoke erupting from the undercarriage. We took it for a quick test spin. It worked fine but for one side effect of the repair: the exhaust was now leaking *inside* the car, and it was apparent any prolonged trip might result in carbon-monoxide poisoning.

"Not to worry!" Strappo proclaimed. He went to his trash bin and produced a large plastic bottle and a length of thin copper tubing. He cut the bottom out of the bottle and handed it to me, keeping the copper pipe for himself. "Breathing apparatus!" he exclaimed. We took Belsen for another test run. We couldn't have clouds of white smoke pouring out of the windows—that surely would garner unwanted attention—but at the same time, we couldn't survive with the windows shut tight. Letting just enough smoke escape from the cab and using the "breathing apparati" through cracked-open windows was the ticket for sucking in unpolluted air.

Melinda had bemusedly been watching the repair fiasco. When she saw the car fill with white smoke, she begged off the trip. No way was she getting in that contraption—the breathing apparatus didn't reassure her at all. She'd hang with Pud and hope Strappo and I lived through our ill-advised journey.

We survived the drive to Bosigran, and the cops never pulled us over. In fact, as long as the car maintained a good speed and the windows were cracked, we didn't really need the breathing devices, though I did have a slight headache by the end of our two-hour road trip. We stopped at the British Mountaineering Council hostel near the cliff, dropping off our sleeping bags and claiming a bed in the bunkhouse, and then hiked out to the top of the seacliff. The Main Wall was a couple hundred feet high, rising from a stone beach. The cliff was a mass of cracks and corners tilted at various angles, and the granite was solid. The routes had a familiar feel, like the granite cracks I'd climbed in Yosemite, and I felt right at home on them.

We had two perfect days of blue skies at Bosigran and climbed until exhausted, our hands scabbed and chafed by the rough granite. Strappo was due to return to work, but the weather remained good, and wasting a day of sunshine in England is an absolutely unforgivable sin. I listened as Strappo called his boss at the bus depot and explained, with complete seriousness, how carbon monoxide poisoning had rendered him too ill to get out of bed. His boss bought the bullshit, and we had another day of lovely granite by the sea, climbing at Land's End.

Melinda and I were anxious to continue our tour. We hitched to Wales and had a taste of the historic and heady climbs there between the almost-daily rain showers. However, the romance of camping in a sheep paddock in Llanberis Pass lost its luster after a few mornings of waking to a sheep-shit mud puddle seeping into our tent. We moved to the Peak District, which was where I most wanted to climb anyway. The Peak has two types of rock: limestone in the dales and gritstone, a very hard, dense sandstone, along the hillside tops, known as edges. In 1981, there was little doubt that the Peak District, along with the few major climbing centers in the United States, held the highest standards of rock climbing in the world. But there were way more Brits climbing than Americans, and the Peak, with the city of Sheffield as its climbing epicenter, held more talented climbers than any other single place on the globe.

Stanage, the largest gritstone crag, was our first stop, with its hundreds of routes of all grades along the winding flanks. The climbs were short, never more than about fifty feet or so, but they made up for their brevity with difficulty and sometimes danger. Protection was frequently sparse on anything but the most straightforward cracks, and the handholds on the face climbs tended to be rounded and insecure, with the footholds even more dubious—just minimal smears a few square millimeters in area. On some climbs, I felt like I was oozing upwards with barely enough friction to stay attached, while other climbs were more simian, requiring pulling on positive holds and moving upside down through overhangs. I loved it. The climbs, with their short, burly cruxes and physical sequencing, reminded me of mini Gunks routes.

Melinda and I made camp on a small patch of weeds at the base of a cliff in Stoney Middleton, the tiny hamlet that served as the gathering spot for the core climbing scene. Stoney was home to The Café, a rough little diner that catered to climbers and truck drivers, and served a menu of English delights, including a "full set" for breakfast (a take on the American bacon and eggs, but on steroids, including baked beans, fried tomatoes, and blood pudding—having this for breakfast assured a climber of a "high-gravity" day and potentially shortened lifespan) and for lunch, maybe a "chip butty"—French fries sandwiched between two pieces of white bread slathered in butter. Melinda and I stuck to beverages.

More importantly, Stoney was the location of an old, abandoned quarry, whose limestone cliffs rise right above the road. It wasn't the most aesthetic climbing around but had a convenience factor impossible to beat. The Brits were friendly and happy to give advice on what to climb. Our mornings started with tea in a booth at The Café, joined by other climbers who'd also "slept rough." At first, I wondered where everyone was spending their nights, because we didn't have tent neighbors at the cliff, then I learned that many of them were bivouacking in a nearby woodshed. One reason for the high performance level of Brit climbers was the "sponsorship" the British government provided. Jobs were scarce, and all the "shed dwellers" were on the dole. Britain was fairly generous to those out of work—at least, generous from the dirtbag climber point of view. If you were willing to live in poverty, then Margaret Thatcher provided just enough cash to make sure you didn't starve. I found it even more impressive that many of these climbers *saved* enough of their paltry monthly stipend to eventually afford plane tickets to the States!

My first climb on English limestone was at Stoney, and it was an eye-opener. I started on a recommended classic called *Wee Doris*. The given grade of E3 6a, roughly translated to the easier side of 5.11 according to my calculation, shouldn't have caused a problem. The route, which climbed a steep wall along its 60-foot length, looked easy enough from the ground. But, in reality, the vertical rock was continuously strenuous, the limestone glassy-smooth. Adding to the insecurity were the footholds slickened to a fine sheen on the over-traveled climb. My forearms got pumped into balloons of lactic acid, and it was all I could do to not fall. I was never so relieved to get to the top of a climb. But I was learning; I was getting better.

In the Peak, there were plenty of climbers to spur me on to my limit. One was a new friend, Nigel. Nigel was a good climber, and a rarity around Stoney Middleton since he actually had a job to go to during the week. He knew the routes and crags inside out, and we quickly hit it off. We had many of the same climbs in mind and teamed up for them on the weekends.

One of them was one of the harder climbs at Stoney, an E5 6b called *Kink*. The toughest moves tackled a bulging roof with a vertical crack, resembling a fat man's belly protruding over a belt. The difficult pull to get established over the lip was not going well for us. I'd just fallen off and given Nigel the rope for his burn when a younger kid, skinny and with a mop of tangled dark curls, came up. The kid grinned as if he knew what was about to happen as Nigel approached the crux overhang. Nigel struggled, grabbing a hold, changing his mind, and then scraping around for another one until finally his arms gave out and he fell.

"Mind if I have a go?" the youth asked. "Not at all, Jerry," said Nigel.

"*Oh, it's* him*!*" I thought. "That *Jerry.*"

I'd already heard news of Jerry Moffatt, then eighteen years old or so. Jerry was making a name for himself by doing the hardest routes in the country. He'd just repeated the thin crack *Strawberries*—E7 6b, or around 5.12+—at Tremadog in Wales. *Strawberries* was one of Britain's most difficult climbs at the time, established by one of its top climbers, Ron Fawcett; I'd failed on it while we were in Wales. I stood back and watched Jerry tie in and then dispatch the roof, using a hidden hold off to one side of the crack that Nigel and I had not seen. He climbed quickly and powerfully, obviously well acquainted with the route, knowing all the tricks for a speedy lap up it.

After Jerry lowered off, I tied in. At the lip, I reached for Jerry's hold. It was a good, reasonably large one. I reefed on it and began pulling over the lip; a moment later, I was airborne. The hold had snapped off as I was getting a foot established, and now it was history. "Guess it won't be getting done with that sequence any longer," quipped Jerry, as he turned away, leaving us to ponder our next strategy. It was the first time, but certainly not the last, that Jerry Moffatt burned me off.

On the very short list of the Stoney Middleton Café's charms was the large collection of dog-eared climbing magazines that didn't circulate in the States. The only widely available foreign climbing journal in the United States was the British title *Mountain*, which put most of its attention on alpinism. And while *Mountain* had some news of advances in rock climbing, that reporting mostly focused on what the Brits were up to in their country. Back home, we had *Climbing*, which covered all the genres in the sport but also retained a national focus, at least in its reporting on new climbs of note from the major U.S. climbing areas. So, without some word-of-mouth beta, those two publications were the main portals to the rest of the climbing world for us in the States.

With plenty of rainy-day breaks and over endless cups of tea, I paged through magazines written in languages I couldn't read and drooled over pictures of cliffs that looked fantastic, with unpronounceable names—sandstone crags in West Germany, limestone gorges in France, granite cliffs all over the place. It was a veritable all-you-can-climb European smorgasbord.

I decided the Rhineland Pfalz in West Germany was as good as anywhere to begin our exploration of the continent's offerings. I hardly understood a word of what the article in the German magazine said, but the area's red sandstone cliffs looked too good to miss. After a long day and night of budget train travel, we arrived at our destination, Pirmasens. The sun shone and we were warmer than we'd been in over a month of "summer" in Britain. The only problem now was, what did we do from here? The magazine article said there was a campground or climber hostel at the "Barrenbrunnerhof" in a small town called Schind, but I had no idea what a "Barrenbrunnerhof" was. Melinda had stayed up much of the night, making sure we got the right trains on our many connections through France. Her fluency in French was key to us getting this far, and she was exhausted. Now that we were here, and this was my idea, she asked, a little tersely, "Okay, *now* what?"

After wandering around a few streets, we found a road sign pointing to Schind and started walking that way. I stuck out my thumb for passing cars. After a few minutes, one stopped. The driver, Michael, said he'd seen my rope tucked under the lid of my backpack. He was a member of the climbers' club that ran the Barrenbrunnerhof hostel, and he drove us straight there.

Michael was amazed that we had come all this way to climb in the Pfalz and treated us like long-lost family. I was used to hospitality from the general climbing tribe—being invited into a climber's home to couch surf for a time or getting treated to a home-cooked meal—but this was over the top. We were fed a huge lunch, which we gobbled up. It had been a twenty-four-hour shift of crap train-station snacks, and we were hungry. Once we were sated, Michael showed us to a private room with a soft bed and clean sheets, as well as a hot shower. Melinda smiled her approval before we fell into a deep nap.

Michael returned in the midafternoon to give us a tour of a popular local crag called the Klosterwand, and put me on a climb he called a classic. Down below, while I climbed, a small throng of elderly gentlemen had gathered, and they stared up at me silently. They were a stereotype of how I imagined geriatric European mountain climbers should appear—some wore traditional alpine hats of a past era, while others had wool knickers and tasseled socks. There was even a guy clad in lederhosen. All that was missing was the St. Pauli Girl. The men nodded with approving smiles after I lowered from the anchors. I'd flashed a UIAA VII—whatever that rating meant. This was yet another grading system I'd need to figure out, but at least I had a benchmark—the climb I'd just done felt like a 5.10.

A few of the gentlemen had obvious disabilities—one had an eye patch, another had a partially amputated arm, and another used a stout cane to help support his prosthetic lower leg. These were all wounds, I surmised, from a war not that far in the past. One of them spoke English and asked about our trip, translating for his friends. I mentioned that we'd just come from England and asked, innocently enough, if he'd ever been there. He paused for a moment before answering, "Yes, I was a guest of the English for some time . . . as a prisoner of war," a slight smile curving his lips. The man took my gaffe in stride, and we steered the conversation to more comfortable pleasantries.

We couldn't afford to stay at the hostel, so we moved to a cheaper campground, a beautiful spot surrounded by sandstone towers, just as the magazine article had promised, with ancient castles jutting from the rim of the cliffs. After the weekend, the German climbers all but disappeared from the cliffs. It was so unlike the Peak District, where Monday morning seemed meaningless to the resident, dole-supported climbing community. However, the few local climbers I did see that week gave me my first glimpse of the revolution that was on climbing's doorstep and changed how I thought about the rules of the game back home.

One of the crags, the Trifels cliff, had a slightly overhanging wall, its smooth face offering a sparse assortment of pockets both small and large. The climbs were protected by expansion bolts, each one a few meters above the last in a straight line. I watched several climbers climbing solo on fixed, single-line topropes, using ascenders attached to their harnesses to keep them in place when they fell. They would hang on their ropes after falling, testing holds and body positions, working the climbs and figuring out the moves—and *not coming back to the ground!* This would have been blasphemy back in the States, where, as you'll recall, if a climber fell he was obligated to return immediately to the ground and start from square one, even if toproping. Still, it looked intriguing, and I wasn't in the Gunks; I was in Europe . . . Did I really need to conform to a norm not practiced there?

I picked out a route on the Trifels cliff called *Zehentanz* to toprope. It was graded IX- on the UIAA scale, or about 5.12b. I had climbed enough 5.12s to know they held one thing in common: they only yielded success at the price of lots of effort and sometimes multiple days of attempts. The climb turned out to be a series of short boulder problems, each of these tougher sections interspersed with decent rests on bigger holds. I fell at each of the harder moves multiple times, but instead of lowering, I had Melinda hold me in place so I could work out the moves until I became comfortable with them.

After successfully linking the moves on toprope, I led *Zehentanz* without falling, moving fast through the well-practiced cruxes and resting efficiently between them. I'd reduced the time to climb a 5.12 from most of a day (or more) to just a couple of hours. How efficient that was! But I also thought it was cheating, like I was robbing the rock, not giving it a chance to properly test me. Where was the small-"a" adventure in this? I'd removed any mystery about what was above the next hold, while the bolts offered solid protection that let me fall with impunity.

After my lead, Melinda said, "Boy—that was quick work!" and gave me a congratulatory hug. I admitted that I was pleased with how fast I'd done a hard climb, even with the questions I held about the tactics I'd employed. There definitely were some major advantages to this new approach—a style that would soon become known as "sport climbing."

Melinda's fluency in French proved handy again, navigating us to the world's oldest, most famous, and presumably best bouldering area, Fontainebleau, a fairyland forest of beech, oak, and pine southeast of Paris dotted with thousands of rounded sandstone boulders. At Bas Cuvier, we pitched our tent amidst huge boulders perched in the sandy soil. Even though I didn't consider myself much of a boulderer, preferring roped routes on "real" climbs, this place was almost too good to be true. There was every conceivable size and shape of rock, beautiful crack lines, arêtes, slabs, steep faces, overhangs—whatever a climber could possibly want. The place may as well have had a large sign that read, "CLIMBERS, COME AND GET IT!"

I wandered the maze of stone, picking a boulder problem here and there to climb, and came upon an old man, looking to be in his seventies but still thin and fit. I watched him effortlessly dance up a holdless low-angle slab. He said something in French to me. Seeing I didn't understand, he motioned to me to have a go. *"No big deal,"* I thought—this septuagenarian had walked up to the slab and made it look trivial. I dipped my hand in my chalk bag, and the old geezer rebuked me with a sharp *"Non!"* Well, I understood that, and I'd been warned about using chalk at Fontainebleau, where the locals instead used small bags of rosin they called "poof." They applied this substance to the bottoms of their shoes and sometimes slapped their bags on the rock itself to increase friction. I abandoned my chalk bag to appease my host.

On my first try I slipped off as soon as my second foot left the ground. Subsequent goes gained a bit more height, but I still skated off the slick surface again and again. To pile it on, the old codger watched me flail with pursed lips, a "Tsk, tsk, tsk," and a slow *"Non, non, non"* shake of his head. He "poofed" his shoes and got back on the boulder, emphasizing each move to show me how simple it really was. I still couldn't do it. I finally gave up, a little disgusted with myself but with Fontainebleau lesson number one under my belt: don't judge a route's difficulty by a local's effort, age, or hairline.

The Fontainebleau forest offered thousands of problems, most of them arranged in circuits. These circuits had been created to help climbers prepare for the mountains, making for a long, hard day of difficult climbing as you moved from outcropping to outcropping, ticking dozens of problems. The modern-day locals usually didn't bother with the circuits, calling them "tourist routes," and instead spent their time on ever more difficult single problems. But the circuits intrigued me. They were graded by colors. Orange and yellow were easiest, followed by blue, red, black, and finally, white. These circuits usually had somewhere between twenty-five and fifty problems that were more or less of a consistent level of difficulty. Orange and yellow ones were easy—moves that were mostly 5.7 or easier. The moves on the blue problems were like cruxes on 5.9-to-5.11 routes. The few red problems I did were downright hard. And I didn't even try any black or white problems.

We bumped into some friends from England back at the campground, and over dinner we decided we'd go for the Bas Cuvier blue circuit, which had forty-eight problems, the next day.

Armed with small squares of carpet to clean the soles of our shoes, and with bags of "poof" replacing our chalk bags, we set out early. We needed to set a time limit for each boulder to make it through the circut before dark, and we needed to climb together so we could spot one another. Crashpads were still a decade or so in the future, and that little square of carpet didn't take much bite out of a groundfall.

The first ten or so problems weren't too bad. Everyone kept up the pace. However, during the next dozen problems, we lost all flow. Maybe it was the caffeine wearing thin, or the rising temperature, but by the time we got to the problems in the mid-thirties, it was every man for himself. We scattered out into the woods, no longer bothering with spotting each other. I started getting smug as I made my way through the problems, now with only a half dozen or so left. Then, I got to the holdless friction-slab nightmare where I'd had my encounter with the old, bald dude the day before. This time, however, I held the secret weapon: a bag of poof. I slapped that slab with the bag like I was beating dirt out of a carpet, and then did the same to my shoes. I walked right up that glassy slab, my feet sticking to the sandstone like a housefly walking up a wall. Some minutes later, when I pulled myself over the top of problem forty-eight, my fingers were flayed to their final pink layer of skin, but I was satisfied. It was one of the hardest days of climbing I'd ever had.

My respect for bouldering increased many notches after that grueling session. Bouldering in the Gunks was something we primarily did at the end of the day or when the weather was being uncooperative. But after getting my first taste of Fontainebleau sandstone, I understood how this could be a passion. I saw how these little poems of movement, distilling climbing to its essence, had a charm all their own—a gravitational force like a black hole. It was easy to get sucked into the moment of pure movement, one unsullied by the distractions of ropes and gear.

Melinda and I traveled south to Bonnieux, an ancient village atop a large hill in Provence. Narrow, cobbled streets climbed past quaint buildings with red tile roofs, perched along the town's steep slopes. The campground showers were free as long as we didn't want hot water, which could be purchased by inserting coins into a box and which proved totally unnecessary amid the

August heat of southern France. We'd come here to explore one of the cliffs I'd read about back at the Stoney Middleton Café, a weird-sounding crag named Buoux. Even Melinda wasn't sure how to pronounce it: "Booh?" she said. We found out it was pronounced "Beeyoux" when we met some British climbers in the campground and exchanged hellos. They had a car and offered to drive us to the climbing the next day.

The short ride to Buoux was beautiful, and I was quickly falling in love with Provence. Groves of olive trees blended into lavender fields that stretched out in neat rows of purple, contrasting with the bright-white and gray limestone cliffs jutting from the hillsides. As we descended into the Buoux valley, towering walls of rock appeared everywhere. It was obvious why this zone, almost unknown to anyone outside of France, was quickly becoming a destination hot spot for the Brits.

I purchased a small climbing guidebook at the restaurant in the tiny hamlet, revealing yet another grading system I had to figure out. The French, like most of the continental Europeans then, used their smaller cliffs for practice climbs, preparing for the big mountains. As a result, they graded their rock routes with the same system they used on the peaks. It was a batch of French adjectives, a little like the British system, only even more unhelpful. Exactly what did *Très Difficile* mean? How *Difficile*? How *Très*? There were a few bolts here and there, and pitons in pockets and cracks, but we needed our rack of traditional gear to do the climbs.

Buoux offered a stupendous smorgasbord of climbing options. Some walls were so festooned with pockets, it looked like they'd been used for target practice by every caliber of firearm. There were long pillars with crack systems that stretched to the rim of the valley, lower-angle slabs of gray rock to test footwork, and orange overhangs to test muscles. And barely anyone was there. What really made the place special to me was the pockets. Slipping a couple fingers into the holes and moving up with powerful pulls was a magic unto itself. When I'd look down to place my feet, it seemed the pockets would vanish, reappearing only when I leaned out from the rock to spot them.

When our fingers needed a break from pocket-pulling, we caught a ride to the Verdon, one of the few French cliffs I'd had in my sights to visit when we'd left the States. At a campground in La Palud we ran into a bunch of folks from the Peak District climbing scene. Apparently, Melinda and I weren't the only ones tired of cold rain and hanging out at the Stoney Middleton Café. In fact, most of the climbers we'd run into in France had been British, not French. I'd even heard that well-known English climber Pete Livesey had once quipped, "The future of British climbing lies in the south of France." Judging from the inhabitants of the Verdon campground, his words were prophetic. Even the guidebook I had for the crags of France, *French Rock Climbs,* was an English one, written by Livesey.

La Palud was a quiet town sitting on the rim of the Verdon Gorge, a deep canyon with gray limestone walls well over a thousand feet tall and stretching for miles along the river that formed them. Buoux, which had looked so large to us at first, now seemed a tiny place. The scale here was vast—more on par with Yosemite Valley. The routes demanded a healthy dollop of commitment as well. Most climbs began with a series of rappels from the lip of the canyon into its depths, to a ledge or stance somewhere above the base of the wall, thereby avoiding a long approach and poorer-quality rock at the very bottom of the gorge. The exposure was immediate and striking. Clipped into an

Melinda Rutledge, En Vau, France, 1981

anchor on a tiny ledge with a void below and many hundreds of feet of smooth, vertical cliff above, I felt miniscule. Melinda was happy to not climb any big routes when she got her first glimpse of what they entailed, so I teamed up with English acquaintances who already knew the place. We had to start early for those big routes, not only for the length of the climb, but to minimize time spent baking in the summer sun.

When she saw my excitement after a few days out on those long climbs, Melinda's curiosity eventually got the better of her. She wanted to do *Luna Bong,* a traditional classic that Livesey's guide gave a Yosemite Decimal System grade of 5.10. The route climbed 150 meters up an overhanging wall, and because of its angle, the approach was infamous—you had to keep a swing going by kicking off the rock as you rappelled in order to not be left stuck hanging in space, The rappel had reportedly sent veteran climbers retreating from their plans before they ever touched stone.

I went first, sliding down the rope. My repeated kicks off the wall kept the swing and momentum going. Toward the end of the rappel, there was a small ledge with a scraggly cedar tree. I snagged a branch with my toe and pulled myself in. Melinda was quite happy to have me holding the ends of the rope to assist her in joining me at the tree. The remaining rappels were less dramatic, and Melinda showed more calmness than I thought she would, given how gripped I'd felt the first time I rapped into the gorge. She climbed the route beautifully, loving every pitch, but the Verdon sun finally took its toll on our motivation to do long climbs in the blistering heat. We were cooked, and our nut-brown skin felt like desiccated shoe leather.

The next evening, we arrived in Cassis, a port town in a

picturesque setting on the Mediterranean. The place was packed with French vacationers taking their August holiday, and the sea lapped lazily against the shore, matching the vibe of the tourists. The street abutting the water was lined with vendors selling waffles, crepes, and ice cream, and customers sat at café tables spread along the sidewalk, enjoying their meals. We walked up a steep hill to the municipal campground and pitched our tent in a small slot between two tiny camper trailers. In the morning, we caught a boat taxi for the short ride into En Vau, an idyllic calanque, a cove of bone-white walls and towers erupting out of the light-blue sea. The boat slid into the inlet and dropped us off on the rocky beach. We spent the day doing easy climbs amongst the sunbathers and throngs of French climbers on holiday, as well as soloing long traverses not far above the water, happily falling off as we got pumped and enjoying the swims in the warm Mediterranean.

Our European sojourn ended all too quickly, and I already wanted to return. Pete Livesey had been right about the South of France: the climbing potential on its limestone cliffs was seemingly limitless. And that was with my traditional-climbing mindset. All the routes we'd done in France had been in "trad" style, placing our own gear and using the occasional fixed piton or bolt. The revolutionary tactics, the "sport climbing" I'd witnessed in the Rhineland Pfalz of West Germany, had yet to cross into France.

I thought a lot about *Zehentanz*, the 5.12 in Germany I'd quickly knocked out and on which I still felt like I'd cheated. Hanging on the rope and working all the moves, using bolts placed on rappel every few meters, just didn't feel like real rock climbing. Yeah, I *did* take pride in climbing that thing fast, but I also knew that if I tried such antics back home, I'd be ridiculed, and my ascent would be nullified as quickly as an Olympian medalist who failed a drug test.

TOWARD THE SETTING SUN; RED ROCK AND GRAY GRANITE

"May your trails be crooked, winding, lonesome, dangerous,

leading to the most amazing view."

—*Edward Abbey*

For several years, my friend Ed Webster had been regaling me with his photos and tales of the perfect cracks splitting smooth sandstone walls in a place called Indian Creek in Utah's Canyonlands area. His pictures of the soaring lines cleaving smooth, brick-red vertical walls made my palms sweat. Especially enticing were his many photos of the route *Luxury Liner*, a.k.a. *Supercrack of the Desert*, a perfect hand crack. Finally, I decided I had to see the place for myself, and put together a trip to the desert for April 1982 and enlisted my buddy Gordon Banks. I planned to pick him up at his home in Aspen on the drive out from New York.

Gordon suggested inviting along a third, a British climber, Brian, whom he'd met the previous summer in Colorado. In the lead-up to the trip, Brian and I exchanged letters several times, and he even shared his climbing résumé with me, down to how many attempts certain routes had taken him to climb. The explicitness of his descriptions made me think he had to be a little over the top and uptight, but nothing unmanageable. At the very least, he sounded motivated to climb hard. I picked up Brian at JFK and drove back to my folks' house. Brian had a typical rock climber build; thin and sinewy, and about six feet tall. All his gear for the trip was in one small backpack. While I prided myself on being able to travel with minimal gear, Brain's pack made my luggage for overseas travel look overkill. I wondered if he had anything but climbing gear in that sack. I soon found he did, but it sure didn't include any food.

Brian mentioned he could use a bite to eat, and I invited him to find something in the fridge. He pulled out some sandwich ingredients and made one for himself. Finishing that off, he went back and made another, and then grabbed himself a beer. When he opened the fridge for a second beer, my mother took notice, telling him firmly but politely that he was to keep his fingers off the beers and buy his own if he wanted some. Brian wasn't put off at all by the light scolding and took it in stride. He went back to the fridge and found something non-alcoholic to drink. I wondered if the guy had ever seen a well-stocked refrigerator in his life.

My British pal Strappo made a last-minute decision to join the trip and arrived at JFK the next night, so Brian joined me for another ride to the airport. We drove back to Mamaroneck, seated across the bench seat of my truck, with Strappo in the middle. He and Brian made small talk about who they each knew back in England, searching for a connection. When that topic wore itself out, Brian, in a weird non-sequitur, enthusiastically told Strappo of all the wonderful food at my house—not only was it abundant, but it was also "free!" Strappo looked at Brian quizzically, and then turned to me and muttered, sotto voce, "What a strange person!" I laughed. Strappo had just given Brian the acronymic nickname he'd hold for our journey: W.A.S.P.

We departed for the West early the next morning, before Brian had a chance to empty my mother's refrigerator. Strappo and I contrived to keep Brian in the back bed of my pickup during the drive as much as possible. It was the only way to keep him quiet. Left to his own devices, Brian would blather incessantly about climbing in such detail even we would tire of it, usually opening these conversations by peppering us with questions. An example:

Brian: "So Russ, what's Indian Creek like?"

Me: "I don't know, Brian. The Wingate formation is supposed to be good sandstone, but I've never been there."

B: "How are the cracks? The pictures of those splitters look amazing!"

Me: "Yes, they do look astonishing."

B: "So what are they like?"

Me: "Like I said, I've never been there. I don't know. You know as much as I do."

B: "Yes, but what do you *think* they're like?"

Me: "I think they're going to be pretty hard."

B: "Do you think they'll be strenuous?"

Me: "Ahh, yeah, I'd guess so."

B: "Do you think we have enough gear?"

Me: "We'll probably wish we had more cams."

B: "So what will we do first?"

Me: "I haven't any idea. Again, I've never been there. There's no guidebook. I have a few pieces of beta from Webster and know what *Supercrack of the Desert* looks like. Aside from that, it's an adventure."

B: "So will we do *Supercrack* first?"

Me: "I don't know. I suppose we'll look around a bit."

B: "Do you want to lead *Supercrack* or shall I?"

Me: "Why don't we just get there and see what happens?"

B: "So would you mind if I led *Supercrack*?"

And so it went, until I'd just turn up the volume on the cassette player to put an end to the interrogation.

Our first night on the road, we pulled off the interstate for a meal at a diner. When the check came, I did the arithmetic and told everyone what to chip in to split the bill evenly, three ways. However, Brian protested and insisted that we each pay for exactly what we had. *Okay, fine.* I re-did the math and told Brian what he owed. He balked again and insisted on double checking. He came up with a different figure. Confused, I took another look. I immediately saw he'd not considered tip or tax. When I pointed this out, he grew angry.

"I am not leaving a tip! I am just paying for my meal!" Brian fumed. However, he'd been to the States before, and surely knew that tipping is a common practice here. I insisted again. He grew even more irritated.

"Listen," he said, "I've already spent too much money since

I arrived, much more than my daily budgeted allowance. I can't afford it!" I wondered what he'd spent any money on so far, aside from chipping in for gas. He'd not bought any food except gas-station snacks and had eaten all his other meals at my parents' house.

"Well, Brian," I said, "we have an issue here. I refuse to take a climbing trip with someone who is going to argue with me about a buck here and there. You can either pay the tip you owe or get out of the truck now." Resentfully, he pulled some change from his pocket. "*Shit*," I thought. "*Am I going to have to arm-wrestle this guy every time I need him to open his wallet?*" My trip to England the year before had given me a good sense of how well those climbers squeezed every iota of value out of a pence, but Brian was taking it to a new level. It was good that Strappo was along, to dilute the need for me to engage Brian any more than necessary.

After picking up Gordon in Aspen, we drove to Moab, which at the time was still a tiny backwater. It had one traffic light, and judging by the lack of cars, its only use was decorative. Along with the light were a post office, two gas stations, and a grocery store. At the store, we grabbed a couple of shopping carts and started chucking the usual climber fare into them: black beans, tortillas, chips, salsa, oatmeal, ramen noodles, canned chicken breast, and big jugs of water. Strappo found an aisle with generic cat food on sale for ten cents a tin, and he grabbed a couple of those to put in the cart.

"What the hell is that for?" I asked.

"Emergency rations," he replied.

"I'm NOT chipping in for *that!*" protested W.A.S.P.

In Indian Creek Canyon, I was thankful for all the photos Ed Webster had shown me of the place, which helped us get oriented. We parked in a turnout by the creek, with the easily recognizable *Supercrack* buttress rising just across the road. We were the only people in the area, surrounded by walls of red rock. As soon as we exited the truck, we bolted like retrievers and charged up the hill to the cliff. I gawked at the architecture of the place. Webster's description and photos hadn't lied; if anything, he'd downplayed the true immensity of the place. Horizon to horizon was filled with buttresses, split by crack lines of every width. It looked endless. We stumbled around, yelling at one another, "Look at this one!" while only paying attention to our own discoveries.

Back at the campsite—a small fire ring in the cottonwoods, encircled by a couple large logs and an old bench seat from a pickup—we found we had a visitor. A van had parked next to my truck, and inside it was a big, muscular dude with a bushy beard, a decade older than any of us. Mugs Stump introduced himself. I knew of Mugs by name—he was a badass alpinist from Salt Lake, his groundbreaking, technical first ascents on Alaskan peaks and in the Canadian Rockies being the stuff of legend. Mugs knew the climbs around Indian Creek and pointed to a few landmarks. He was on his way out of the area, but before he split, he gave us friendly advice on where to climb.

The next morning, we hiked over to the Fringe of Death Canyon, relying on Mugs' recommendation. All the crack lines looked long, steep, and difficult, with hardly anything good to warm up on, to stretch out our limbs and get the blood flowing. We eventually found something we agreed looked suitable, a friendly-seeming, rather generic crack that would fit my hand size well for secure jams. Years later, I'd find out that the crack was, indeed, named *Generic Hand Crack* and was a 5.10-. We piled all our Friends together: in Indian Creek, where the cracks can stay the same size for a ways—even a whole pitch—multiple cams of the same size are extremely helpful. However, we had no more than four or five pieces of any one size, which meant we'd have to supplement our cams with passive protection in the form of Hexentrics. I started up, sinking my hands deep into the fissure and wedging and twisting my feet in as I progressed. Every ten feet or so, I stopped to place a piece of protection; by the fifty-foot mark, I'd used up all the Friends. Now I was wedging in the Hexes, which took a lot more time and energy to place and were far from ideal in the parallel-sided crack. I was getting ever-more pumped, and by the time I reached the anchor, forearms swollen and sweat cooling on my brow, I vowed to buy more Friends, despite their cost.

Every climb we did was a complete mystery. Aside from *Supercrack*, we didn't know the names or grades, and would only know if a crack had been climbed before if we came to a lowering anchor partway up the cliff. In cases where we didn't find anchors, we created our own after completing a pitch, which we ended either at a ledge or a stance, likely making the first ascents of these climbs. After Mugs left, we didn't see another climber aside from some friends from Aspen who joined us. We had this astonishing, vast place to ourselves, which, in the modern era, would be all but unheard of. Once in awhile, a car would drive through on the road below, but other than that, the only noises we heard besides our own voices were the occasional yelp of a nocturnal coyote and the sighing of the desert wind.

Besides the multitude of cracks on the buttresses, there were also grand towers soaring up hundreds of feet above the desert floor. Gordon and I went to do *Lightning Bolt Cracks* on North Six Shooter Peak, a 5.10+ route Ed Webster had established a few years before and told me was a "must-do" climb. The four-hundred-foot obelisk was split by various crack systems, but picking the right one wasn't hard: it resembled its namesake, a couple cracks zig-zagging up the face. Gordon and I swapped leads, making our way toward an imposing overhang guarding the summit. Happily, the overhang was more bark than bite, and only 5.10, with a good hand crack skirting its edge. We remained quiet on top of the tower, gazing at the desert stretching to the snow-white La Sal Mountains under an endless blue sky, both of us content.

After about ten days, the blissfulness faded and dissent was in the air. Strappo was getting sick of being in the desert and of the brutal cracks. They had taken a toll on all of us. Our hands and fingers were beaten to a pulp, despite the protection of the athletic tape we meticulously applied each morning, bonding it to our hands with our little brown bottles of tincture of benzoin. Plus, the very social Strappo could no longer bear going to bed

Strappo savoring his cat food burrito

before 9:00 p.m. and seeing no one else but our little group. To top it off, we'd run out of beer.

"If we don't leave here, I'm heading out by myself for Boulder!" he proclaimed. My first thought was, *Good luck!* I could count the cars that had passed by our campsite during our entire stay on both hands. It would be a long wait for a ride. But Strappo was serious—which, for him, was rare. He proclaimed he'd walk to the main road if he had to. The rest of us, in need of a break as well, relented and agreed to make our way back toward Colorado.

On the way, I had one climb I badly wanted to do. The volcanic plug of Shiprock, on the Navajo Reservation in New Mexico, was listed as one of the "Fifty Classic Climbs of North America" in the book of that title, which had recently been published. There was one problem, though. I'd heard from some climbers that it was illegal to climb Shiprock and that we might be trespassing. Other climbers I knew said it was not a big deal and no one cared, but there were also rumors of climbers being caught, chucked into jail, getting fined outrageous amounts, and having their gear confiscated. I related these tales to Strappo as we cruised south through the flat, scrub-filled desert. Strappo was concerned. W.A.S.P. didn't seem to mind, as long as it wasn't going to cost him money. And Gordon was his usual analytical self. I asked him what he thought. He pondered the plan a few moments and declared the odds of being busted as low. We were going for it.

Shiprock erupts dramatically from the high desert. It looked to me like a giant sailboat, a highly featured and complex mountain, with many ridges and gullies splaying off its central axis. It rises over other similar, but much smaller, volcanic features, like a king above its minions. I turned onto US 666, which Strappo took as a very, very bad omen. He was also growing ever-more nervous about the potential trespassing aspect of the climb.

"You don't suppose we'll be caught, do you?" Strappo asked.

"Are you serious, Strappo? C'mon—what are the odds? There's nothing around us and nobody out here," I said.

Closer to Shiprock, we pulled off the main road onto one of the dozens of small dirt tracks leading toward it. Along the way, we found that the "flat" desert topography in fact contained plenty of washes and gullies in which to park and hide. With the truck invisible from any nearby road, we felt safe from discovery, and even Strappo had calmed down. As I started up the stove to cook yet another meal of bean burritos, Strappo pulled a busted-up, barely functional chaise lounge from the truck—a relic he'd grabbed from a roadside trash heap when we'd stopped for gas. He plopped himself down and began to eat a burrito of his own.

"What are you eating? I'm still cooking," I said.

"I've had it with bean burritos! Bloody sick of bean burritos. I won't eat another bean burrito!!! I've tapped into emergency rations!"

There beside his throne was an empty tin of the ten-cent cat food, and as Strappo munched happily away, I caught the heady aroma of dredged seabed. Long after he finished his supper, the lingering stench of rotten fish guts wafted from his craw every time he spoke. The rest of us teetered on the verge of losing our own dinners.

"Strappo, you gotta wash your mouth out with something—

have you ever shot a beer?" I asked.

It turned out he hadn't, so I filled him on the procedure: punch a hole in the base of the beer can, apply your mouth to it, suck in to create a vacuum, and then turn the can upright, pop open the top, and shoot the beer from the hole. This is best done with tin cans, but the cheap swill we'd picked up after leaving Indian Creek came in aluminum cans and we didn't have a decent can opener, so we resorted to using a pocketknife to create the hole. Strappo sucked hard, popped open the can, and instantly had a corner of his upper lip pulled into the jagged orifice. Beer spilled from his mouth, along with trickles of blood. We all laughed uproariously and even Strappo found it amusing, but then he asked us to stop laughing as it was making him laugh and extending the wound when his lips tightened to smile. Eventually we all calmed down and Strappo freed his only superficially damaged lip.

We woke at first light, wolfed down breakfast, and racked up. Gordon said he'd climb with the W.A.S.P., and I teamed up with Strappo. Just as we were ready to head to the rock, we heard the rumble of a truck engine above our campsite gully. We stripped ourselves of our gear and stashed it under some bushes. I climbed cautiously up the slope of the wash to take a peek. I stuck my head over the top, just enough to see the intruders. Two guys were approaching, ropes over their shoulders and gear clanging from their harnesses. When I emerged from the gully, they jumped in shock, turned on their heels, and ran away. When they stopped to check if I was following, they realized I wasn't a threat. What came next was a footrace to the climb. No one wanted to be behind a possibly slower party. Strappo and I got to the base of Shiprock first, with Gordon and W.A.S.P. right behind us. The other climbers had decided to either leave or give us time to get ahead. In any case, we never saw them again.

The route turned out to be easy and fun. A small bulge with a 5.6 move at the very start was the only impediment before we entered a long stint up a large, shaded groove on low-angle, questionable rock. The holds on the shattered basalt were big and plentiful, but not always trustworthy. We had to take care in picking the best ones. We didn't bother roping up, and without the need to set up belays, felt the freedom of climbing fast. It was like being inside the mountain rather than on it, well hidden in the deep gash of a three-sided elevator shaft. We soon emerged onto the upper, sunny reaches of Shiprock, with a panoramic view of the desert floor a thousand feet beneath us. The rock here became a more solid volcanic tuff. One thousand feet up, I was no longer worried about being spotted by anyone looking for climbers. At best, we would look like tiny dots, even through binoculars.

We roped up for a couple of short, technical sections to the summit, where we logged our names in the summit register. As we downclimbed, we passed by Gordon and W.A.S.P., and agreed to meet up back at the truck. Strappo remained nervous while we waited, even though we hid all our climbing gear under some bushes. He only relaxed as we drove away from Shiprock later that day.

Melinda met me in Aspen when we dropped Gordon off after our desert foray. I'd missed her more and more as the trip wore on, but I didn't realize how much until we hugged and I looked into those glacier-blue eyes and felt her warmth. She was ecstatic to be away from Boston, and I couldn't have been happier. Our relationship had weathered the previous winter with regular visits on weekends, meeting in the Gunks or her place in the

Boston suburbs. We were both living in our parents' houses to save money for exactly this purpose, and this outing would be the first long hang since our last trip together in Europe.

Melinda was well acquainted with Strappo from previous trips, but the W.A.S.P. was new to her. She had listened to me complain and make fun of him when I'd called her before we disappeared into Indian Creek, but Brian had since mellowed a lot, settling into the rhythm of the trip and becoming less intense, less verbal, and a lot easier to hang with. Our time in Indian Creek, where there were no options for spending any money, had probably helped: he hadn't complained about finances in awhile. My tolerance also increased when I realized I had some mellowing to do myself. I'd been pretty hard on him, and once the money thing stopped being an issue, I liked Brian more. He was quirky, but also amusing once you got past the overly earnest climbing talk. We had tied in together at Indian Creek often, and he'd proven himself a pretty good climbing partner.

All four of us—me, Melinda, Strappo, and Brian—wanted to visit Red Rock Canyon (a.k.a. Red Rocks), a reportedly excellent climbing venue outside Las Vegas. There was very little written information about climbing at Red Rocks at the time, and certainly no guidebook, though I'd heard stories of big sandstone walls, limitless crags, and boulders galore. We stopped in at the outdoor shop in Vegas to see what we could learn, but the two indifferent, if not outright hostile, salespeople there—who, judging by their dirtbag-casual attire and rough hands, were climbers—had nothing more to offer beyond a perfunctory, "You guys might want to head out to Willow Springs. You'll find some stuff here." I left the shop pissed off at the snub. It was the first time I'd encountered such lousy hospitality at a climbing area, especially at a shop that should have wanted my business. And in fact, I did need some chalk, but there was no way I was going to give them a cent of my money.

We left for Willow Springs in the heat of the late-April afternoon, driving out West Charleston Boulevard, a two-lane road that rapidly left behind the growing city. Miles of empty desert stretched in front of us, bracketed by huge, pyramid-like formations of red and brown rock in the distance. As we came closer, we found ourselves overwhelmed by the complexity and size of the area—by its deep canyons and unending walls. Yes, there was a ton of rock, but where to start? And where the hell was Willow Springs?

We followed the road in its loop around the park, eventually coming to the Willow Springs Picnic Area. There, above the parking lot, sat a small bluff of what appeared to be reasonably good sandstone with a slick, black veneer. But there were no other climbers about—no one to ask for beta. We climbed a few short routes, which were easy and nothing special. It was also hot and unpleasant, but mostly it seemed so stupid to be climbing fifty-foot cracks when we had towering walls all around us—about which we unfortunately knew nothing. Clearly there was excellent, abundant climbing here, but the only way we were going to get to climb anything significant was with local knowledge, and we didn't know anyone to turn to. It would be another couple of years before the first guidebook was published, and all we could do was stare up at the big walls. We split the Mojave for cool mountain air, tall conifers, and granite.

It was dark when we reached the town of Idyllwild in the San Jacinto Mountains in Southern California. We parked below the large domes of Suicide and Tahquitz silhouetted against the night sky, rolled out our sleeping bags under the Ponderosa pines, and slept well in the chill air. In the morning, the first route I just had to do was the mystical *Valhalla*. The route had a reputation as a hard and scary slab climb, with two pitches of 5.11-. A successful ascent allowed membership into the fabled clan of the Stonemasters, a group of leading SoCal free climbers that included well-known names like John Bachar and John Long. I knew the reputations of some of these "masters" since they were in the climbing press regularly, with their ascents on California granite. Becoming a Stonemaster had been a big deal in the 1970s, but I wasn't sure it meant much now, in 1982, or if we were even candidates since we weren't Californian. Thus I wasn't surprised when Strappo and I topped out *Valhalla* to zero fanfare, no locals waiting around to knight us as the official Stonemasters Sir Russ and Sir Strappo, perhaps with an anointing bong hit.

Our next stop was Yosemite, where our group split up to climb with new partners. Our personal agendas varied per the routes we wanted to do, and perhaps we'd had enough of each other's company after two months together on the road anyway.

I wasn't seeing much of Strappo while I climbed with others, but he was keeping busy. While I climbed Half Dome with another friend, I'd missed one of Yosemite's more entertaining evenings. Strappo had been hanging out in the Mountain Room Bar, conversing with some patrons over drinks, when the subject of nudity came up. Strappo asserted his complete comfort with his naked body in public places. To prove his point, he stripped down, jumped on top of the bar, and streaked across it. When he reached the end, he turned for a return lap, bumped his head onto a ceiling beam hard enough to make him lose his balance, and fell onto the bar. The crowd gave him a rousing round of applause when he got up. Strappo took a bow and put his pants back on. I was bummed I'd missed this historic event. That had to be a first, even in Yosemite.

Not long after, Melinda had to go back home to work. Yosemite was getting hotter and more crowded by the day, so I was ready to move on too. The W.A.S.P. decided to linger in the Valley, and so did Strappo. Then Strappo hit a wee bit of trouble one night when he decided to reprise his bar-streaking stunt. Unfortunately, the second act wasn't received quite as well. One of the patrons at the Mountain Room Bar that evening was an off-duty law-enforcement ranger who didn't find Strappo's antics the least bit amusing. Strappo spent the next four days in the Valley hoosegow before he appeared in Judge Pitts's Yosemite Village courtroom. His honor didn't find the streaking stunt any funnier than the arresting officer had. Judge Pitts declared: "Mr. Hughes, you've climbed the walls, climbed the bar, climbed the tables and chairs. It's time you left." Strappo was ordered to not darken Yosemite National Park with his presence for at least one year. But Strappo stayed on anyway, disguising himself with dark sunglasses and a long trench coat, seeking refuge in Tuolumne Meadows, where he successfully hid out.

I'd read an article in *Summit* magazine about a place in central Oregon called Smith Rock State Park. It was difficult to believe there would be anything worth climbing in the middle of Oregon, but the photos in the article looked amazing, especially one of a climber in the middle of a long, smooth-walled corner called *Sunshine Dihedral*. I was solo when I left the Valley, and that picture was a magnet, drawing me to explore Smith Rock.

The view over the rim of the Crooked River Gorge at the tall beige, brown, and red walls was stunning. The river coursed lazily through the little gorge, its shores dotted with slopes of junipers and sage that rose directly to the cleaved architecture of the many cliffs. However, it was hot here in the high desert—really hot—in mid-June. The sun beat down on my head like a molten hammer as soon as I exited my truck, and I didn't see any other climbers around. Still, when you're traveling solo, you've got to pack some optimism in your luggage. I pulled my climbing gear out and took the footpath down into the gorge.

The rock, a welded tuff, is essentially solidified volcanic ash, and as I walked along the base of the cliff I wondered about the integrity of the stone. I tested a few holds and they felt nothing like they appeared. I expected them to explode when I pulled on them, but instead they were solid, small, and sharp. I wandered by the big corners of the Dihedrals Area, stopping below the one I recognized from the magazine, *Sunshine Dihedral*. There was some evidence of it being climbed recently, with chalk marks in the corner crack and on the smooth walls. That afternoon, I did a few pitches with some locals who showed up—wisely—after the east-facing cliffs dropped into the shade, and got a feel for the rock.

The next morning, in the cooler temps, I went back down to the gorge to, I hoped, find someone to climb with. At the base of the cliff, two guys were bouldering to warm up. One was spotting his partner, a thin guy with brown hair who looked to be around my age. The spotter glanced my way as I watched, but kept his concentration on his buddy until he finished the problem. The climber, Alan Watts, stepped over to me and introduced himself.

I recognized him from the magazine article as the guy climbing *Sunshine Dihedral.* Alan was happy to give me a tour of the area, showing me the classic crack routes like *Sunshine Dihedral, Karate Crack, Shoes of the Fisherman,* and a grab-bag of others, many of them his own first ascents. I worked my way through his list during my stay, starting with the easier ones, mostly because I was uncertain about the rock and the ability of my gear to hold a fall. The welded tuff did feel solid, and I never had a hold bust, but could the force of a fall break a nut placement? When I finally did take a decent lob on one of Alan's recommended routes, my fears abated: the piece held fast.

Besides the existing classics, Alan unveiled his plans for lines he planned to climb in the future. Smith was a total backwater, and Alan and a small circle of regulars had the place to themselves, with little competition for first ascents. His aspirations and appetite for new climbs were enormous. One future route he showed me was an awesome-looking overhanging arête jutting over our heads, with a sharp, 90-degree edge that looked like it had been cut with a jigsaw. Alan said the climb would be incredible, and I couldn't help but agree. *Incredible for sure,* I thought, since it was obviously going to be very hard and probably impossible to protect. There was no crack line to follow—no place to insert protection. All the existing routes Alan had shown me so far were crack lines and corners that took gear, but these blank-looking faces and arêtes had none. Sure, I could see pockets here and there, and with some imagination string together a continuous line of them, but they would be death routes.

I looked up at the arête that would later be known as *Chain Reaction* and figured Alan was either delusional or suicidal. In fact, *Chain Reaction* would soon become the poster child for sport climbing in North America, symbolizing the revolution in rock climbing about to hit the continent like a roundhouse kick to the head.

In 1982, the concept of sport climbing was completely foreign to US rock climbers. American climbers placed gear in natural features. We started from the bottom and worked our way to the top, dealing with the unknown as we ascended. Sport climbing, with its prior inspection of the climb and bolts placed on rappel—eventually with battery-powered rotary hammer drills that let you blast in a bolt hole in seconds, not the painstaking minutes it took with a hammer and hand drill—was not considered true climbing in America. And forget the idea of hanging on the rope to rehearse the moves after you fell: that was also flat-out cheating. You had to return to the ground and start all over. Even in Europe, where I'd first witnessed it the year before, sport climbing was only just beginning to take hold. But because Smith Rock was obscure and had such a small population of climbers, Alan could do what he wanted without fear of repercussions. He became the godfather of sport climbing in the United States and lived on one side of a developing schism in the American scene.

Through the 1980s, many American rock climbers wanted to hold onto the traditions of the past, highlighting boldness as a crucial part of the challenge. Rock climbing had by now divorced itself from the idea of being practice for mountaineering. It was a recognized end in itself, but it was still regarded in the same family, much like siblings share DNA. So, the concept of "fair play"—giving the rock a chance to defeat the climber—meant following one of the principle mountaineering rules: start from the bottom and let boldness decide how far you climbed. As rock climbing matured in the 1970s, climbers graduated to using only "clean" protection, like cams and nuts, eschewing pitons altogether to protect the resource. And to really preserve boldness, a climber should never, ever, ever place a bolt unless absolutely necessary.

The new sport-climbing ideal didn't give a rat's ass about boldness and danger, or about old rules of engagement that made sense in the mountains but that—if you stepped back to consider them objectively—seemed stupidly contrived at the crags. Sport climbing was all about pure difficulty, and the results justified the means, as far as the new wave was concerned. Sure, closely spaced bolts and rehearsing sequences took the boldness away, but they also allowed climbers to push the difficulty envelope to a degree never before seen—and much more quickly. When I left Smith after a week of climbing the classic routes Alan had suggested, I wondered about his dreams and if Smith Rock would ever be more than a backwater, second-rate area. Despite what I'd seen and experienced in West Germany just a year earlier, I just couldn't imagine that ever happening in the States. Little did I know what a clairvoyant Alan was.

THE WIZARDS OF OZ AND TASMANIAN DEVILS

"Every country is like a particular type of person. America is like a belligerent, adolescent boy; Canada is like an intelligent, 35-year-old woman. Australia is like Jack Nicholson. It comes right up to you and laughs very hard in your face in a highly threatening and engaging manner."

—Douglas Adams

Melinda was ready for our relationship to get more serious. We were both tired of taking turns driving between Massachusetts and New York, as we'd done through much of 1982 when not on the road climbing together. She took a job with a brokerage firm near my folks' house and moved into an apartment of her own. I was still intent on saving every dime I could for more climbing plans and remained at my parents' house when I was working. I was happy to have Melinda nearby, but I was also worried—I had a packed agenda. I would be going to Australia in a few months, leaving in early February of 1983, and I'd be gone for four months. She knew that and we thought it would be okay, at least on paper; we still loved each other. Unfortunately, reality hit as my departure drew near. With me away, there wasn't any social glue to bond her to Mamaroneck, and it would be lonely for her there.

Melinda wasn't one for big arguments, and instead let her displeasure show by growing ever quieter as my trip approached. We avoided the topic of Australia, but it filled the air around us, and our time together became stilted and uncomfortable. Perhaps I was being a selfish asshole for leaving right after she'd moved, but I wasn't going to give up a trip I'd been planning for a year. I rationalized my position, even though I felt pangs of guilt and knew I'd miss her.

Australia was the beginning of the end of our four-year relationship, but I was blind to that. Even in the last couple of winter months before I left, I was still focusing on doing new routes up in the Gunks. I'd leave early on Saturday mornings to meet up with my friends. If the sun was on the rock, so were we. And if it wasn't, we did wind sprints up and down the talus slopes to warm up before jumping on the rock and getting a burn in before our hands and toes froze. Melinda sometimes came along, and sometimes she didn't. Her enthusiasm for hanging out in the cold only went so far.

After my flight landed in Sydney and taxied to the gate, the captain told us to remain seated. Airline personnel came aboard to cleanse the aircraft of any undesirable microbial hitchhikers and sprayed insecticide, filling the cabin with a poisonous fog. I covered my mouth and nose with my shirt and tried to breathe as little as possible. My initial thought was, *If this is an Aussie welcoming, I'd hate to see what they do if they're pissed at you!*. My disinfected jet continued to Melbourne, where I called Kim Carrigan and met him and Louise Shepherd at the outdoor shop where he worked. It was great to see them again, and nice to see that they'd remained a couple since I'd last seen them, almost three years earlier.

The pair were off to Mount Arapiles for the weekend with their friend Robin to climb at this storied Australian crag, and the biggest reason I wanted to climb in Australia. When Kim had been in the Gunks, he couldn't stop boasting about the rock quality of "The Piles," comparing it to the Gunks. I also knew that Henry Barber spoke highly of the place after leaving his mark there in the mid-'70s, establishing the country's hardest free climbs at the time. Arapiles remained ground zero for Australian rock climbers testing the limits of difficulty, and was a traditional climbing bastion, much like US centers.

Unfortunately, I wouldn't fit into Robin's tiny car for the four-and-a-half-hour trip, so they scurried me off to catch a train to Horsham, a town about thirty miles from Arapiles. They'd pick me up there for the last leg to Arapiles.

The Pines, the Arapiles campsite, was exactly that—a grove of tall pine trees that provided comforting shelter for climbers' tents. The last hints of dusk were about gone when we arrived, so I stumbled around in the gray light looking for a likely patch of dirt to call home for the foreseeable future. As soon as I got my tent up, I crawled into my sleeping bag, totally jetlagged, for a long-overdue rest.

Early in the morning, staccato laughter jolted me from my deep sleep. I experienced one of those disorienting moments when you're not sure where you are or how you got there. I would learn my cackling friend was a kookaburra. That bird became my daily cuckoo clock for my stay. A few moments later, I heard a *thump, thump, thump* and opened my tent door just in time to see a kangaroo's bobbing tail disappear around a bush. Now I was wide awake! I got out of the tent, eager to start the day, but the rest of the campground was still asleep, so I explored.

I'd heard Arapiles resembled a giant pile of horse dung. Now that I was seeing it up close, that description was laughably accurate, but I could also see that there was *a lot* of terrain. Gullies split the formation in all directions, with tall walls on either side of them. It looked user-friendly; there was something familiar about the place. I walked to a nearby boulder, its surface streaked with brown and reddish tints. I stroked my hand along the fine-grained quartzite and grabbed onto some edges. They were sharp and positive, just like Gunks holds, and right then I knew I was going to love it here. I wanted to start yelling and wake everyone. Instead, I continued my exploration. Steep crack lines and face holds caked with chalk revealed which routes were the most popular. The more I looked, the more excited I became to climb. While checking out one particular route, I noted a couple of the infamous "carrots" I'd heard about. Instead of using proper expansion bolts, like the ones placed occasionally in the States on the crackless sections of traditional climbs, Australians bought regular old bolts from hardware stores. These were exponentially cheaper than "real" bolts. They'd file down the threads to taper the bolt (creating a "carrot"-like shape) and hammer it into a drilled hole. In order to clip a carabiner into the carrot, Aussies used a specially manufactured bolt hanger, designed to slip over the hex-head of the bolt. They carried these hangers in their chalk bags, inserting and removing them as needed. Word was, the carrots were solid, but I wasn't in a rush to take a whipper on one.

Back at camp, Kim, Louise, Robin, and I discussed the day's plan over cups of tea. Kim had an agenda.

"It's going to be blazing hot, so we'll head for shade. It's one of the nice things about Araps—you can find either sun or shade depending on what you need. We'll go up to the Trojan Gully," he said.

Louise looked at him with a wide-eyed expression. My sandbag radar began pinging immediately.

"Kim," she asked, "do you really think that's the best place to go for his first day at Arapiles?"

"Oh yeah," Kim said. "There's plenty to get on up there, and *Trojan* is a classic."

"Yes," she acknowledged, "but it's also bloody hard!"

"How hard is it?" I asked.

"It's graded 25, but I can give you the beta and you'll be fine. Hardest bit is right by the bottom. You'll love it," Kim assured me. The Australian grading system, the Ewbank Scale, required minimal alchemy to translate to my American grades. It simply used an open-ended numerical progression. In this case, I knew 25 was somewhere in the hard-5.11 or easy-5.12 range—far from a warmup, especially with the crux at the bottom. At the time of my visit, the hardest grade in Australia was 28, or 5.13a.

"Is there anything easier?"

"Sure. There are a couple classic 22s [5.11s] and the like up there too."

Of course, it turned out this gully was also the home of Kim's latest project, *Masada*, a route he'd been working on for some time that would eventually become the hardest rock climb of the era at Arapiles—and the real reason we were headed to this particular spot.

After we did a couple of pumpy warmups, Kim got to work on *Masada*, so named for the ancient fortress in Israel that successfully repelled repeated invasions. *Masada* and *Trojan* shared the same boulder-problem start, so I got to see Kim float up it before he moved left onto his project, taking an even steeper line up a series of small corners and arêtes. I fell into a much-deluded opinion of the difficulty of *Trojan's* entry moves. It didn't look so bad. But it was. When I eventually conquered the start, I spent forever resting in a large pod just twenty-five feet off the ground, warily eyeing the overhanging crack above. A few moves later, I fell and lowered to the ground. I'd gotten a proper ass-kicking, and *Masada* had once again stood firm against Kim's advances. We left the gully in the dwindling light of the late afternoon, defeated but smiling. *"I'm climbing in Australia!"* I thought. I was happy, despite Kim sandbagging me.

After the weekend, the Pines emptied out. Kim, Louise, and Robin left, along with most everyone else, aside from the few dirtbag residents. The 100-degree heat of the peak Austral summer was awful, and the wind sometimes whipped up the dust, making it essential to find a sheltered gully for climbing. Despite the conditions, I did a lot of climbing with the locals who were ensconced at Arapiles. One in particular was keen for any outing.

Malcolm "HB" Matheson was a nerdy engineer-type, always happy to discuss gear and how to improve it. He had what I thought of as a "farmer's physique": a thick, muscular frame and sturdy legs, and a wispy mustache he perhaps hoped made him look older. The only thing more boundless than HB's enthusiasm for climbing was his ability to talk about climbing. He was always ready to climb another pitch or sell you one of his homemade "HB" cams. These were beautifully designed pieces of art, essentially small Friends made with titanium, long before cams to protect cracks smaller than one inch became commercially available. Undoubtedly, he was in violation of at least a few patents, but nobody was coming after him. His cams were used by everyone around Arapiles—they were perfect for the area's tight seams—and I bought a couple right away.

HB was a little younger than the core group and a comparative climbing novice. As a noobie on the Arapiles climbing scene, he wasn't held in high regard by the better climbers, even though, being from Horsham, HB was maybe the only true local. But Horsham was considered an out-of-touch cow town and its residents a bunch of hicks by the urbane Melbourne crowd who frequented Arapiles. When HB was his given nickname by the "in" crowd, Malcolm was honored. To him, it obviously meant that the others had noticed his climbing prowess and were reminded of the great American climber Henry Barber. However, Malcolm didn't realize HB stood for "Horsham Bruce" (in Aussie slang, a "bruce" is a man), a snide reference to his backwater origins, though even after realizing the jab he good-naturedly embraced the moniker.

Almost all the younger Australian climbers were locked onto punk culture with open arms. Climbing for many of them was a way of giving the finger to the establishment and to societal expectations. They loved the sport and its anti-materialistic, fringe lifestyle and culture. It wasn't unusual to wake up in the Pines to Jello Biafra or Jonny Rotten screaming punk lyrics from someone's ghetto blaster, or to have my partner for the day sporting pink hair and brightly colored pants. Also, in the tiny Oz scene, every climber knew every other climber, as well as their business. There were no secrets about who was sleeping with whom or who had his or her eye out for someone else. It was

The gang at Lost City, the Gunks: Kevin Bein, Colin Lantz, Russel Erickson
(left to right) circa 1986

amusing and safe being on the outside looking in, and even if I'd wanted, there was little chance to get any romance started. There were precious few females, and those who were around were like ripe bananas to fruit flies.

We welcomed a new arrival to the Pines, someone Carrigan had met at his shop in Melbourne, fresh off a flight from Japan. Kim said that Takashi had stood silently in the store, perusing guidebooks, until Kim asked if he needed help. Takashi said, in a heavy accent, "*Awapaweez.*" Kim tried to figure out what Takashi wanted to know about Arapiles, but Takashi's English pretty much started and ended with that one word. Kim gave him directions and a map to the train station and sold him a guidebook to Araps. Either Takashi wasn't fond of trains, or he couldn't find the train station. But he did find the correct roads out of Melbourne and spent four days hitchhiking the 200 or so miles to the crag. When he finally got there, no one could understand a thing he said. The resident Aussies dubbed him "Tennis Shoe," their best shot at interpreting his name. Tennis Shoe wasn't a very good climber when he arrived, but he was strong, and quickly got better. He was also smart, and his English improved rapidly, to the point where he was soon making rejoinders when the Australians mocked him. I thought about the trip I had made to this end of the earth, and what it took to get here. Compared to Takashi, coming from a completely different culture and a country with little developed rock climbing and no knowledge of English, I was a punter.

One of the most colorful members of the tribe was Michael Law. Michael was an intensely bright and gregarious guy, and had been nicknamed "Kinky Claw" or simply "Claw" by the climbing community. I never asked why, nor did I want to know. In appearance, he was the anti-Kim Carrigan—softer and less fit than the training-obsessed Carrigan, but blessed with heroic finger strength and wicked determination. One of Claw's many talents was sewing, and he fashioned his own garments from whatever remnants he found at local fabric houses in Melbourne. When he made a protracted visit to the States later that year, his eye for fashion sparked the lycra craze that hit US crags in the '80s. While that phase of climbing fashion didn't last long, it did make for colorful photos in the magazines of the era.

Claw took me to a handful of local crags he'd developed around Melbourne and sandbagged me on his under-graded creations. A fave of Claw's was a route he called *Belt Your Kids*, which was the tagline of a public-service ad to remind parents to make sure children were using seat belts. At the crux, instead of the standard fixed protection like a bolt or a piton, Michael had affixed half a seat belt—the feed mechanism—to the cliff. With your feet well above the last piece of protection, you had a choice: grab the seat belt out of fear or clip your rope into its metal eye as protection and then try the moves. If you clipped the seatbelt without grabbing it and fell, it would act just like it would in a car; the sudden jolt would lock it up. However, if you chickened out and grabbed the belt, it would extend, sending you plummeting onto the piece below.

Michael introduced me to Chris Baxter, the publisher/editor/writer/office manager for the two Australian outdoor magazines, *Wild* and *Rock*. Chris was a lot older than me—in his late thirties. He was a towering figure, well over six feet, with a trim black beard and close-cropped hair on a gigantic melon of a head. In fact, his nickname was Melonhead, and he owned a bellowing voice that announced his arrival well before his actual appearance. He loved telling tales of the two rival factions in Australian climbing, the Foxes (anybody too old to lead anything hard, himself included) and the Ferrets (the younger set who now warmed up on what the

Foxes had deemed the difficult climbs of their day). Chris took great pleasure in relating sagas about how the old Foxes would take advantage of the young Ferrets' naïveté by cajoling them to lead up dangerous and difficult terrain. It seemed to not dawn on him that this would be just what they wanted as a way of proving their superiority over the previous generation—but never mind.

Chris lined up a trip to Tasmania for a few weeks with three of his buddies and invited me to join the gang. One of them, Glenn Tempest, was known as "Trumpet," so-called, said Baxter, for "blowing his own horn." Dave Moss, a.k.a. "Chubba," came from Queensland and been named for his less-than-Olympian body shape. While the nicknames struck me as insulting, Glenn and Dave were unphased by them, just like those Aussies I'd met in at Arapilies. I began to think I was being left out of the inner circle without some kind of disparaging sobriquet.

The final member of this junket was an old friend of Baxter's from England, Miles. Miles was about Chris' age, and they climbed at about the same level. Since Glenn and I were also of similar age and ability, we ended up teaming up for many routes. Dave acted as a go-between. His level of climbing fell between the old guys and the young ones, but his heart was with the youth. It was the Ferrets versus the Foxes.

We took off to climb at a backcountry area containing a couple of sizable volcanic walls, Mount Geryon and the Acropolis. This pair of large crags only had a few routes at the time and had only been visited by climbers once before. It took us a day and a half of hiking on muddy trails, lugging our heavy packs, to get to our destination.

When we got to Geryon, the sky was filled with a misty haze, the peak's summit disappearing into the clouds. Geryon's east face was about 1,200 feet high and broken up, while the shorter south face of Acropolis was roughly 800 feet but much sheerer, with cleaner rock. Both cliffs featured a columnar structure reminiscent of Devils Tower in Wyoming. They rose over a lush green valley in a storybook setting, and I half expected to see a troll or elf wander through. We set up camp at the base of Mount Geryon, finding a recess in the cliff with an overhang for protection, just big enough for the five of us and our gear to mostly stay out of the drizzle after we cleaned out the remains of a desiccated wombat. It was easy to imagine in this pristine setting that we were the first human visitors.

Chris was drawn to the immensity of Geryon, while Glenn and I were lured by the Acropolis, with its more continuous crack systems. The climbing turned out to be really good: the lower part of the cliff was a little less than vertical and fairly easy climbing, but higher the wall steepened and the cracks thinned, going from solid hand jams to fingertip-sized fissures. Over the course of the next week, Glenn and I did new routes, freed old aid lines, and brought the Acropolis into the modern age. A couple of our climbs would be oft-repeated classics, especially *Astroboy*, an excellent crack-climbing extravaganza we rated 24, were they not such a slog from civilization. But then again, the lack of civilization was why we were here. From our belay stances, we could see Chris, Dave, and Miles, dust specks on the mass of Geryon, and hear their belay calls echo across the lonely valley.

Eventually our luck with the weather evaporated and rain came in hard. I wondered if anyone would ever go back to the Acropolis and repeat any of the new climbs Glenn and I had done. I didn't really care one way or another. We'd had a great time soaking in the solitude of that backcountry wilderness, and I knew it was a place I'd never see again. There was then, and remains with me today, a melancholy mood when I leave a place I've thoroughly enjoyed but know in my heart I'll not likely be back to visit. There's only so much time, too much rock and way too much world to see.

I got to back New York, unsure of where my relationship with Melinda stood. I had written letters to her while I was gone, but only heard back once. When we got together for the first time since I'd left, we were awkward, like two people on a blind date trying to feel each other out. I wasn't sure how to act and didn't want to talk about my trip. That would be picking at a scab. Even so, for a couple months, we went climbing together and tested the waters to see if there was anything left. There wasn't. Melinda told me she was quitting her job and moving to Vermont. We both knew we were just friends now. The energy we'd need to salvage our relationship, if that was even possible, simply wasn't there.

HOME IS WHERE THE OVERHANGS ARE; BRINGING THE GUNKS UP TO SPEED

"There's no place like home."

—Dorothy Gale, *The Wizard of Oz*

The youthful Gunks talent pool in the early 1980s created cliques of three or four people who tended to stick together, though intermingling was common when there was shared interest in a certain route. Jack Mileski was often out with Mike Freeman, the sole Black climber in the area. They were up every weekend, rain or shine. Jack, like Freeman, was also from Jersey, and was a treat to watch move on rock. He wore his dark hair long and shaggy, and always had his stash pipe at the ready for a hit at the end of the day. Great technique and an acute kinesthetic awareness brought Jack through difficult sequences with seemingly little effort. He was also the most creative linguist in the climbing world, and would make up verbal descriptions of climbs that sounded like garbled word salad. "Yeah, ya gotta bone on the chacal piss, tweek into the Sawicky, then gaston into the vista cresta with the left paw, hit the volcanic board, and it's in da bag, Spencer!" he might say, describing the crux of a climb, incorporating words that made obvious references—perhaps likening certain holds to climbing paraphernalia like ice axes—and dredging others from the deepest recesses of his mind.

One of the many terms Mileski coined was "beta," now part of the everyday lexicon in climbing, used to describe how to do the moves on a climb or, more generically, for any information, as in the "camping beta" for an area. His idea came from the original Sony Betamax video recorder. Jack's "recording" mind would "hose you down" and "spray" you with the "beta" about which holds to grab and which sequence to use.

Jeff "Bones" Gruenberg was another regular, a svelte anatomical diagram of human musculature who had us all feeling guilty at a dinner table if we dared to dab butter on a slice of bread. Shit, if you dared touch the bread, Jeff's response was a look of reproach. The "light is right" adage didn't apply to just using the lightest gear available. We trimmed down our already-thin bodies for any edge in our strength-to-weight ratio. Most every top climber at the time was getting as skinny as possible, but Jeff took it to an extreme, getting down to sub-140 pounds with a fanatical training and diet regime, all on a six-foot-two frame. Even more impressive than Jeff's dogged work ethic was his willingness to go for it. I'd never met a bolder climber, and I was happy to let him take the lead on many of our first ascents.

One example of Jeff's fearlessness was a first ascent we made at Sky Top in the early winter of 1983, just before my departure for Australia. *Talus Food* was so named for the jumble of jagged rocks littering the base of the climb, just waiting to eat anyone who fell. The smooth, orange wall was impossible to ignore, but we had been doing our best anyway, passing by it with eyes averted. The wall was almost totally crackless, meaning protection would be either thin or nonexistent, which had been enough to kept

"Ordeal by Fur," Sydney Seacliffs, Australia

suitors away. Additionally, we worried about the quality of the stone. Gunks rock is normally incredibly solid, but when it's deep orange in color—"over-kilned," in Mileski-speak—it's a warning, a yellow light flashing "CAUTION!!!" But eventually, we couldn't ignore that damned piece of cliff any longer and busted out the rope.

Jeff stepped up to the base, tied in, arranged his gear, and climbed. He found good protection at first, solid nuts and a cam in a crack about fifteen feet off the ground. That gear kept him safe for a hard section getting around a small corner system capped by an overhang. Now he stood on the face proper, feeling for edges on the almost featureless stone, and finding just enough holds to keep ascending but no further protection. Soon, Jeff was a good fifty feet above the deck with those first gear placements down low now as useless as a condom on a eunuch.

Jeff reached an impasse and stalled, feeling out the poor edges above and trying to decipher a sequence. He fondled a small flake with his left hand, just the very edge of his fingertips digging in for purchase, and started to weight his left foot. Midway through the move, the handhold snapped and Jeff began to swing, slowly barn-dooring out away from the wall. Then, in a gravity-defying maneuver, he stopped his rightward swing, reeled himself in, and stayed put. Mike, Jack, and I gasped; we had been about to see our friend die. But he didn't. Still, downclimbing wasn't an option—the moves were too hard—and up was the only way out. After a long break to calm himself, Jeff made it through fifteen more feet of precarious moves to a small ledge and finally, good gear. That day, the talus would have to go hungry.

Lynn Hill's arrival on the scene the summer of 1983 added more talent to the Gunks' formidable gang of climbers. I hadn't yet met her but knew her reputation as one of the best female climbers around. She made the trip from California for a magazine article profiling her, and got partnered up with the Gunks' other Russ—Russ Raffa—for the photo shoot. Raffa was a regular partner of mine, and certainly the better of the two of us in my first couple years of climbing with him. He had male-model looks, with slightly curly dark hair, olive skin, and brown eyes. It didn't take much to imagine him on the cover of *GQ*. I was working on a new route in the Trapps when Lynn arrived with Raffa to do *Matinee*, a hard 5.10 that afforded an easy setup for photos. I watched from a shared ledge as Lynn climbed smoothly and quickly through the difficulties.

Lynn stuck around for the summer and instantly fell into the fold of the top climbers. She had us entranced with her personality and ability. While the Gunks had seen its share of good women climbers over the years, from pioneers like Bonnie Prudden in the early years to the more present-day Barbara Devine, Kevin Bein's talented wife, Lynn was different. She didn't see herself as a "good woman climber"—just as a good climber. She took her fair share of the leads, had a determined focus, and knew herself and her ability well. Lynn garnered our attention for other reasons too. She was cute, smart, and carried a forthright, confident air; not surprisingly, she had no lack of suitors, me included. Despite my best efforts, I was no match for my friend, Raffa. He was better looking, had more money, and, to top it off, he had a house in the Gunks. Lynn found a home at Raffa's place.

One climb both Lynn and I wanted to do was the classic testpiece *Supercrack*. Even though its first ascent had taken place in 1974, it was still considered the hardest route in the Gunks, and only a tiny handful of Gunks locals had managed to climb it in the ensuing decade. Lynn and I set to work on it one July day in 1983. We yo-yoed the rope up the crack bit by bit, following the ethic of the time, starting from the ground after each fall. We didn't succeed that day, but we came close. We went back a couple days later and completed our task, elated with our ascent. Just as we were finishing up and cleaning the gear off the route, Raffa arrived with a serious expression on his face, certainly not reflective of the mood Lynn and I were in. He gave us a tepid, "Congrats," and then broke the terrible news that our British friend Pete Thexton had died on Broad Peak in the Himalayas. Pete's death shook me. My buzz about doing *Supercrack* evaporated instantly.

Pete had been a favorite partner as a regular visitor to the Gunks, not only for the climbing but also for his flowering romance with a local lady, Beth Acres. Thexton was instrumental in helping me be a better climber—on my last trip to Yosemite Valley, his positivity, patience, and support got us up the multi-pitch testpiece *Astroman*, an exposed, intimidating climb we'd finished right at dusk that magical day. We endured an unplanned night out under the stars while we waited for dawn to come and light the complicated descent.

I had suggested bailing after we'd done only four pitches that morning, dealing with cramped forearms and dwindling psyche. "Listen," Pete said, "I've done lots of big routes. You've just got to go one step at a time. There's nothing to worry about. We can always go down. So, let's just keep going up." *Astroman* had been crucial in showing me just what I was capable of if I pushed my body past the point where my mind said, "Stop!" That night by our little campfire on the summit had brought us closer together.

Back in New Paltz, a group of us gathered at a friend's house

Pete Thexton on "Astroman," Yosemite Valley, 1982

for a celebratory toast to Lynn's and my success on *Supercrack,* but that rung hollow considering the grim news. Instead, we talked about Pete, retelling stories late into the night.

The year before, in October 1982, Thexton had dropped a rope down an alluring, sixty-foot white wall in the Near Trapps to check it out. British ethics being a little different from ours in the Gunks, he decided it was okay to preview the route on rappel and try it on a toprope first, before daring to lead it. Ordinarily, this would have met with harsh words and heckling from the locals, but Pete didn't care. Plus, there was no one around aside from Pete and his belayer on that cloudy, cold day until I walked in, unnoticed. I silently watched Pete work the route, falling in a couple places but continuing to the top. When he saw me standing there, he asked if I wanted to give it a whirl.

Now, this wall was considered a "last great problem," and all "last great problems" in the Gunks were like mythical quests. Respecting them meant doing them properly: from the ground up, no previewing, no toproping, no hangdogging or any other defiling antics. The line begged to be climbed, but hadn't yet been because the protection looked horrible and the moves looked hard. An existing climb to the left, a very difficult one from the Stannard Era, was named *To Have or Have Not.* With this new climb's potential lethality, we'd already named it *To Be or Not to Be.*

I hesitated at Pete's offer, but I was curious, and the proffered toprope was tantalizing. Besides, hadn't I already tasted the forbidden fruit of working climbs two years earlier in West Germany? And hadn't I found that method incredibly efficient and rewarding? I tied in, feeling like I was doing something mischievous, and surprised myself by flashing the route, getting through the hard bits with the benefit of Pete's beta. I felt both guilty and elated at the same time—just like I had on *Zehentanz* when I'd had my first taste of "cheating."

In early sumer 1983, Raffa and I became obsessed over leading *To Be or Not to Be* and making it a "proper" route, trying it on several occasions. But there would be no more shenanigans like toproping or sussing out gear. It was back to the tried-and-true yo-yo style. As we progressed up the climb, we found there was gear on it—just enough to make the first hard moves safe. After that crux, Raffa placed a marginally secure Friend in a flaring pocket. Above, we encountered moves of unprotected 5.10 climbing for fifteen feet, leading to a point where moves off two small sidepulls—vertical holds—put us into groundfall range, even if that iffy Friend in the flare didn't pull out. We kept backing off, carefully downclimbing to the Friend and lowering to the ground. Unless there was some good protection following the next move above our highpoint, a grounder was a certainty if the leader fell. I scarcely remembered the moves from the previous autumn, much less if there was any chance of good protection. When Lynn arrived on the scene, we invited her along for the fun.

Late on a July afternoon, long after the sun had left the cliff, the three of us were back at it. Conditions were pretty good—a reasonable temperature and bearable humidity for a Gunks summer day. It was my turn to go up, and I could feel the pressure building. I was leaving the next day for a climbing trip, and I had no doubt that if I didn't do it this day, Raffa and Lynn would snag the prize in my absence. Knowing this, I started up, intent on going to the top. Raffa sensed my mood through my determined movement. As I worked into the sidepulls, ready to make the next moves into the unknown, he warned, "Clune, don't do it—it won't count anyway since you toproped it!"

Russ had a point. I had already violated the rules, so why keep going and risk my ass with a potential groundfall? *But if that cam is good, and I'm pretty sure it is . . .* I made a snap decision. I looked down at the cam, assessed the amount of rope out from it, shouted, "Okay, falling," and let go with the perhaps idiotic goal of testing whether the cam would hold a lead fall.

The plunge put my heart in my mouth, but when I stopped about thirty-five feet lower, the cam had held and my tucked legs cleared the ground with a few feet to spare. "There!" I said. "It's safe!" Raffa tied in next. He made the move off the sidepulls, got a couple of good edges, fished a small wire behind a flake, and continued to the top. It was a great lead that Lynn and I followed. *To Be or Not to Be* was an instant classic, at least on a toprope. Even to this day, at a formidable 5.12a R/X, it rarely gets led.

Gunks climbers continued to find plenty of new lines after the 1980 Dick Williams guidebook was published. Many of the creations were scary, with crap protection, and some measured into the high end of 5.12, but often these climbs contained hard boulder problems followed by great rests. So far, none had really overtaken *Supercrack* for pure continuous difficulty, and we were searching for a genuine 5.13. It would be Jeff Gruenberg and Jack Mileski who found it.

Jack christened the climb *Vandals*, even before setting foot on it. Jeff and Jack spent considerable effort clearing the landing of ankle-busting blocks below the poorly protected, difficult opening moves—a minor ethical breach. Then they got to work to unlock the starting sequence, just as I happened by—and joined in. The opening moves were hard, weird, and awkward, and the landing was still not that great. No one climbed higher than ten feet to some small flakes, where we attached skyhooks, small

Frank Minunni on "The Sting," 5.11+, the Gunks

question-mark-shaped pieces of thin steel, used for aid climbing and manufactured to only hold body weight. The hooks were "protection" in name only; a fall would be an injury-inducing backward flop onto the ground when those hooks popped, as they undoubtedly would.

Soon Lynn came along, and we convinced her to go for it. We were strong lads and could surely catch her tiny frame if she wobbled off. Lynn, as is her way, tied in and promptly fired the moves. She then climbed easier rock to a small ledge about twenty feet off the deck, where she inserted a few Stoppers in a crack, the first legitimate protection so far. The rock above bulged for a couple body lengths before meeting a fifteen-foot overhang with a thin, jagged crack breaking its length to the lip. The bulge looked difficult and the path to the overhang unclear. Lynn felt around for holds, trying a couple sequences before deciding to let someone else try. The next possibility for protective gear wouldn't come until the roof.

On my turn, I made the moves to the roof only to find myself with one hand on a fingertip edge and my feet pasted to crappy footholds. I focused on a small crack at eye level, trying to make a nut, any nut, stick in the damn thing. Nothing fit, and my fingers began to wilt. I looked down between my legs for a moment to check how far it was to those last nuts. "Shit!" I muttered to myself before a yell to Jeff, who was belaying me. "I'm off!"

When I fell, I missed the ledge but slapped the wall below it, slightly spraining my ankle. Jeff went next, busting through the bulge to where I'd fallen. He hung on long enough to place two small wired nuts in the overhang. Wasted with the effort, he yelled "Take!" I pulled in slack as he gently weighted the gear, hoping the pieces were solid. They held, and we were in business.

Now we could get to work on the big roof.

We soon had another addition to our *Vandals* party: Hugh Herr. Hugh was an immensely talented climber who'd returned to the Gunks climbing fold after a harrowing epic on Mount Washington, New Hampshire, that had caused him to lose both legs below the knees to frostbite. Hugh made use of different lengths of prosthetic legs for whatever a climb demanded, and he climbed about as well as anyone. As it turned out, that tragic event would eventually lead Hugh to far greater things. He later became a famous, paradigm-shifting inventor of bionic limbs, running a department at MIT. On a more amusing note, occasionally Hugh was accused of cheating by other climbers, and his simple quip was, "If you find it so advantageous, feel free to cut off your own legs."

The four of us went to *Vandals* sporadically over the next several weeks. We'd figured out how to climb the big roof, employing a contorted twist of the body and a particular sequence of handholds to get a good hold two-thirds of the way out, where we could sink a solid cam for excellent protection. From there, we could reach the lip of the overhang, but the holds there sucked, all of them slanting the wrong way and spitting us off into the void only to return to the ground to try it all over again.

At last, I managed the perplexing moves and squirmed over the roof, standing up above the lip with my hands wrapped around a large flake. A bulldozer couldn't have pried me off that hold. Jeff let out a war whoop of victory. My head was level with the belay ledge; it was an easy step up, but when I moved my foot, I was suddenly airborne. The top edge of the flake had snapped off and I fell, still clasping the book-sized hunk of rock. I couldn't believe it, but now the code had been cracked. We knew how to grab the shitty holds at the lip and maneuver through the overhang. Jeff sent it on his next try, and the rest of us led it as well. The four of us knew *Vandals* was a lot harder than *Supercrack*. The Gunks, and the East, finally had a 5.13 rock climb, done in the traditional manner.

While Lynn had moved into Raffa's house in New Paltz, she still had ties to California. Many of her belongings remained there, along with family. She went back over the December holidays in 1983 to visit, and planned on staying with her old boyfriend, John Long, at his apartment in Santa Monica. We made plans to meet while she was out there and do some climbing. Lynn picked me up at LAX and we went back to John's apartment. I'd never met John before, but certainly knew of him and his reputation as a Stonemaster and first ascentionist of some of the hardest climbs in Southern California, such as the horrendously wide roof crack, *Paisano Overhang* on Suicide Rock. John freed that beast of a roof at 5.12 in 1973, wearing a pair of leather gloves to protect his hands and going feet-first out the roof in a then-futuristic technique.

John sat at his desk in the large, open living room, talking in his big, booming voice with his friend DB. John acknowledged Lynn's return with a quick "Hi" but nary a glance, much less a word, tossed my way. "Largo," as he was commonly known in climbing circles, was indeed quite large. Not like an offensive lineman, but more like a middle linebacker, with a huge torso, wide shoulders, and thick arms and legs. The apartment was sparse, holding just the essentials for living. Climbing gear was strewn about, with some climbing books and magazines scattered across a coffee table. I bided my time looking through the climbing rags.

After a bit, DB took his leave and Largo turned his attention to Lynn and myself. But before saying a word, he grabbed the large bong that stood on his desk, packed a bowl, and fired up. After a long tug, he leaned the bong toward me, gesturing I partake, but I smiled and waved off the offer. Lynn did the introductions, and Largo showed some interest in what had been going on in the Gunks. Lynn and John had been in a relationship for years and had an easy way between them, but at this point they seemed more like two siblings than past lovers.

John suggested a trip to Mount Rubidoux, a hillside covered with granite boulders and a favorite bouldering area for Los Angeles locals. As soon as we booted up, Largo began testing me with problems he'd done many times, seeing if I was worth my salt. I would have been more intimidated by this legend, a climber one generation my senior, had it not been for Lynn's presence and encouragement. I tried hard to keep up with Largo and not fail his entrance exam. At first, Largo said little to me, aside from a few words about a problem like, "This is a classic!" while dancing up a glassy face. John cranked out the problems with prodigious power, which was no surprise, and supple grace, which was— especially for a guy who looked like he belonged in a boxing ring, not on slick granite slabs. As the session progressed, it appeared I did all right. John lightened up as we bouldered, tossing jokes and smiling more. My feelings of intimidation melted away with the setting sun. This guy was a blast to hang with.

John's friend, DB, and some of his family were taking a long trip to the South Pacific and needed someone to housesit and care for their pets. John volunteered, and let Lynn and I know we'd be movin' on up. We soon found ourselves standing in front of a huge gated mansion. I was assigned charge of the large guest house, home to a colony of felines, while we all took turns taking care of

Stanley the poodle, a pampered pooch with finicky eating habits and an annoying habit of digging up the well-tended gardens and shrubs. The instructions for Stanley's care were to feed him at certain hours, appropriately time his walks to his feeding schedule, and above all, make sure he did not burrow into the shrubbery.

While the house was nice, I hadn't come to California to hang in Beverly Hills. I itched to get out and climb, and said as much. So, in his charming Largo way, John somehow talked Lynn into watching the house and taking care of the dog while he and I took off for Joshua Tree. We rolled into the Hidden Valley Campground— the main, central hang for climbers—on New Year's Eve 1983. The gang present was a contingent of some of SoCal's finest climbers: John Yablonski, a. k. a. Yabo; Mike Lechlinski; Mari Gingery; Russ Walling a. k. a. "the Fish"; and others. We welcomed in 1984 with beers and bong hits, and fell asleep on the sandy ground, with the wide desert sky twinkling above.

The morning dawned perfectly clear and still. Gossip accompanied coffee and a hasty breakfast as the posse got ready for action. The Southern California climbing scene was well known for being insular and not overly accepting of outsiders. Trash talking about other climbers from anywhere outside the group was a sport in itself; hell, even if you were in the family (but were not at that moment around), there was a good chance you'd get a substantial ribbing. Amid the chatter, I was well aware of my interloper status, though the fact that Largo had brought me along meant I was in—at least for the day.

Suggestions got tossed around until someone decided we should hit a small roadside crag to start. We drove to a short block full of vertical cracks. The routes were about forty feet high, but

I didn't see anyone breaking out a rope. Apparently, free soloing was on the agenda. We started out with easy climbs, solos from 5.4 to 5.9. I was comfortable with that. As we warmed up, the solos became more serious—5.10s and even a couple 5.11s, fortunately with their bouldery cruxes near the ground and easier climbing above.

We moved to the Hidden Valley area, scurrying up slabs and cracks like a pack of baboons and having a great time. Finally, one of the gang busted out a rope to try the famous 5.12 *Leave It to Beaver*, twin cracks that snaked up an overhanging wall to a bulging panel of varnished stone. I was immensely happy to see that no one was figuring on soloing this difficult route today. Someone recalled a story of Yabo's solo of *Leave It to Beaver* a year or so before. Yabo was a legendary risk taker, having lived through mishaps that should have killed him but for some kind of divine intervention. In one instance, he was soloing a forty-foot 5.11 crack, *Short Circuit,* in Yosemite. At the top of climb, he lost it and pitched off, only to be saved by a tree branch that broke his fall and bent enough to lower him to the ground, shaken and bruised but alive.

On his *Leave It to Beaver* epic, witnesses recalled that he'd scampered up the thing as solid as could be, making it look like child's play. Back at the base, super-charged with adrenaline. Yabo declared the route a simple jaunt, and to prove it, he jumped back on for a second ropeless lap. This time, however, was not nearly so solid. The onlookers said they had to turn away as Yabo shook his way to the top, barely remaining attached to the small face holds at the climb's upper crux, forty feet above a tilted rock slab.

When the toprope was set in place, the ends dangled far from the rock, revealing just how overhung the climb was. A nervous shiver ran through my body while I started the process of assessing the moves, trying to decipher the beta. No one asked if I wanted to go first, and I was grateful for that. I watched attentively as someone well acquainted with the route tied in and artfully climbed the thing. I noted where they rested and the sequence of holds they used.

"You wanna go next?" I was asked. I was fully aware of being under the magnifying glass, and I *really* didn't want to fall. Standing there amidst a collection of California's best climbers, I needed to prove that Eastern climbers were up to snuff. It wasn't just for me—I was representing my gang, my fellow Gunkies. I climbed carefully, mimicking the movements of the previous climber. *Leave It to Beaver* went smoothly and felt easy; I'd sensed there was an expectation that I'd fall, and was so glad I didn't. We wrapped up the day with more solos, not quitting until the sun sunk below the horizon. Largo and I left Joshua Tree to return to the mansion, my hands and fingers sore from jamming the rough quartz monzonite cracks all day long, but my climbing appetite sated from what had been a glorious feast of gravity-defying movement in this high-desert paradise.

When we got back to LA, Lynn was ready to do some climbing herself and to let Largo do the house-sitting. A couple of years prior, she and Largo had done the first free ascent of a multi-pitch face route in Red Rocks called *Levitation 29*. She'd spoken highly of the route when we were back in New York, and I wanted to do the climb. Lynn and I drove to Las Vegas and stayed with her friend Wendell Broussard, who, unlike the cooler-than-thou climbers at the local gear shop on my previous visit, was more than happy to spray info about the climbs. I was excited to go back and do what was supposed to be a classic long route, especially in the company of two people who knew the place well.

Wendell woke us while it was still pitch-black outside, since we had to make use of the scant winter daylight. We parked at the trailhead for Oak Creek Canyon, where it was just light enough to make out the shadowed outlines of the huge walls looming in front of us. I stayed warm in the chill air, building a light sweat hiking up the sandy washes and drainages, eventually working our way up low-angled slabs of brightly colored sandstone crisscrossed with stripes of red and brown to the base of *Levitation*. Lynn and I sorted our gear, racking up a dozen quickdraws for the many quarter-inch bolts and a small selection of Stoppers while Wendell and his partner went to climb another nearby route. The height of the brown-and-red sandstone expanse above me was difficult to judge until Lynn pointed out the first couple of belays, where I could see slings at the anchors and get a sense of the scale. I was glad for the early start.

The climbing was a mix of cracks and face holds, never very hard but consistently interesting. I was surprised at how positive and plentiful the face holds were. Now I understood the appeal of Red Rocks—the climbing was just plain fun. Lynn and I swapped leads and moved steadily, completing the eight pitches of *Levitation 29* in a few hours. At the belay for the final pitch, we had a decision: either rap off or do a pitch of easy climbing and then suffer a long hike back down in our tight climbing shoes. It wasn't a difficult choice. We rappelled and were back at our packs by early afternoon. It was the fifth ascent of the route, and a wonderful way to celebrate Lynn's birthday, which just happened to be that day. Aside from Wendell and his partner, we didn't see another soul in Red Rocks the entire time.

We drove back to California the next day, content with our climb of *Levitation*. However, our light mood soured the minute we opened the door to DB's family mansion. There, we were

Lynn Hill on "Levitation 29," Red Rocks, Las Vegas

greeted by a mess resembling a frat house the morning after a toga party. The kitchen counters and sink were filled with used dishes, pans, and pots. On the living-room carpet stood a pile of dog shit, a turd pyramid topped with a dusting of white. Snowstorms in Egypt? No. A cat or two had gotten into a box of climbing chalk and scattered its contents. Outside, the garden looked like a scene from the trenches of World War I: Stanley the poodle had been busy. Lynn and I were horrified, but Largo didn't seem to think it was any big deal. We could wash the dirty dishes, vacuum the chalk, and I'd get to work filling the holes in the garden. Just as we started, we had an unexpected guest: DB's sister, who was not on the family vacation and who'd decided to pop in to see how everything was going. The look of abject horror on her face is not one I will ever forget, nor will I forget how, in one outstandingly long sentence, she colorfully used a favored expletive as a noun, verb, and adjective to describe the scene and render her opinion of John and Lynn as people: "WHAT THE FUCK HAVE YOU FUCKING MOTHERFUCKERS FUCKING DONE HERE AND WHO THE FUCK LET THE FUCKING DOG DIG UP THE FUCKING ROSE BED AND IS THAT FUCKING DOG SHIT ON THE FUCKING CARPET?!!!!!!" Then she noticed me sitting off to the side, and, catching her breath, directed the totality of her ire at me: "AND WHO THE FUCK IS *THIS* MOTHERFUCKING ASSHOLE?!"

GO EAST, YOUNG MAN; A TRIP BEHIND THE WALL

"From Stettin in the Baltic to Trieste in the Adriatic, an iron curtain has descended across the Continent."

—*Winston Churchill*

I found a cheap flight to England early in the summer of 1984 and beelined it for the Peak District. After a few days of climbing, I met up with my friend from New Paltz, Beth Acres. She'd moved there to live with Pete Thexton and remained in Sheffield after Pete's death on Broad Peak, and now had a new boyfriend, Bob. Pete's death had left Beth in a dizzy spell. At first, she didn't know which path to take, but ultimately settled on staying in England, where she found the atmosphere comforting and had the support of Pete's many friends. Now, her relationship with Bob supplied a new framework upon which to rebuild her life.

Our conversation lightened up from remembering Pete and turned to climbing plans. Bob told me he and Beth were off to Czechoslovakia in a couple of days. There, they'd be climbing on the fabled Adršpach-Teplice rocks, a sea of sandstone towers in Bohemia, known for their beauty, long runouts, and strict local ethics. Among the ethical considerations were a ban on gymnastic chalk and allowing only knotted nylon slings for protection.

Bob had been there several times in the past, and said it was an amazing place, a country filled with fun people and gob-smacking stone. Beth encouraged me to join them for their journey. I'd nearly gone years earlier, but that plan fell apart when it emerged that the visa application was a time-consuming and expensive pain in the ass in the United States. However, Bob assured me, the visa was cheap and easy to obtain in London. I could do a bit more climbing in the Peak District, and then after getting my visa meet him and Beth at the campground just outside the village. I scribbled the instructions on a bar napkin with a stub of pencil and tucked it into my pocket.

A week or so later, I caught a bus to London and went to the Czechoslovakian consulate. There, the attendant told me I would be required to change a minimum of fifteen US dollars a day into the Czech currency during my visit and that I'd also need my visa stamped each night by the government-run campground I'd be calling home. I had two choices for the seven-hundred-mile train ride. Like always, it boiled down to time versus money. The expensive train ride would get me there in about a day, but the cheap one, at less than half the price, would take a full two days. I bought a couple extra paperbacks to help fill the time and arrived in Prague bleary-eyed after forty-eight endless hours of bumps, jolts, and connections that didn't allow for sleep, aside from the times when a train would halt, for no apparent reason, in the middle of nowhere. The Czech border was an especially long stop while the customs officials went through everyone's papers and, occasionally, their luggage.

I passed the day in Prague with a young Polish woman who'd been sitting in my train cabin. Even with just a few words of English, she was my savior, helping me figure out which train I needed to take to reach Adršpach later that day and find a bank to exchange my traveler's checks for Czech koruna. We found a pleasant outdoor café on a square for breakfast and sat for a long while over our meal. After breakfast, we strolled. I'd never been behind the Iron Curtain before, and it was shocking to see the difference when we checked out a few shops. Inventories consisted of basic living essentials, and not even much of that. There was nothing to spend money on. In England, I'd wondered if the fifteen-dollar-per-day required exchange would be sufficient for living. But our substantial breakfast had cost almost nothing—a couple bucks at most—and my train ticket was less than a dollar.

A couple stops down the tracks on my final train ride, a young man and woman about my age entered my car and sat across from me, plopping their rucksacks down next to their feet. The guy's pack sported a rope, drooping over the sides under the top lid. As they chatted, he pulled out what I figured was a climbing guidebook, though I had no idea what the cover said. I asked if they spoke English. In response I got only thin smiles and a, "No, only little bit." Then I pointed to their rope and again got smiles and nodding heads, with a "You?" I nodded back. We attempted more communication, but it was unwieldy. I sat back in my seat, too travel-weary to gesticulate my way through a conversation. I'd soon be with Beth and Bob anyway, and spent the remainder of the train ride gazing out the window at the rolling, conifer-filled hillsides.

The two climbers departed the train before the station where Bob had told me to get off: Teplice-nad-Metuji. At my stop, I stepped onto the platform in the dwindling twilight, feeling very alone, like I'd been dropped off in a ghost town. I caught the sound of laughter—a woman and a man sat at the other end of the platform talking. "Do you speak English?" I asked. They did not, and seemed peeved that I'd interrupted their conversation.

I shouldered my pack and walked away from the train station, toward what I guessed was the center of town. All the buildings along the cobblestone streets had been shuttered for the night, and there was nobody about to ask for directions.

In a few minutes time, I came to a cluster of buildings housing a busy bar, with blinking lights scattering off a disco ball and loud dance music pumping out the doors. I figured there was a good chance that Bob and Beth might be here—it was the only place with any sign of life. I stashed my pack in some bushes and went inside to look for my friends, communicating to the doorman through pidgin sign language—a finger to my eye, circling my hand in the air—that I was only looking for someone, and not staying. However, my friends weren't there, neither boogying on the smoke-filled dance floor nor sitting at one of the tables.

Now it was dark and I still had no idea where I was going. Plus, I needed to get to the campground that night to get my visa stamped, which ruled out an open bivy in the woods. I continued walking down the narrow two-lane road coming to a fork at the far edge of the village. A small sign with a tent symbol on it pointed down one of the lanes. A wave of relief hit me, as if I'd been running it out from a last piece of gear and finally reached a good stance and bomber protection. If I didn't find the campground, what were the consequences? I didn't want to find out. I picked up my pace toward the campground, vaguely recalling Bob saying it wasn't far from town.

Out of nowhere, a glow of headlights pierced the darkness behind me. I jumped to the edge of the road in self-preservation, instinctively flicking out my thumb. The car sped by at good clip then screeched to a halt, the driver slamming into reverse hard enough to grind the gears. He stopped next to me with his window down. "Do you speak English?" I asked. Negative. In desperation, I put my hands up and signaled with an inverted "V" and said "Campground?" He said, "Ah! Camping!" and signaled for me to get in. He saved me a couple miles of extra hiking at the cost of a slightly harrowing drive.

The campground operator didn't speak English either, but he had the process down cold. I handed over some money and my passport; he gave me a ticket for a site and stamped my visa for the night. I found an empty space, set up my tent, and then set out looking for Beth and Bob. My first look around was fruitless. On my second lap, I stopped at a site with two guys sitting at their lantern-lighted picnic table, the dim light revealing a rope on the ground. The pair, it turned out, were climbers from East Germany, and one of them spoke some English. There was no other campground in the area, he assured me, and this where all the climbers stayed.

Early in the morning, I did another sweep and still didn't find Beth and Bob. I returned to the East Germans' site and once again verified there was no other campground in the area. Seeing my bewilderment, they made me breakfast and invited me to join them for a day of climbing. They said they visited the area often and could show me around the towers.

We wound our way up sandy paths through fantastic spires of all shapes and sizes. The gray-green rock faces featured flakes, tiny pockets, hueco-like hollows, and the occasional crack. While I pondered the lines on the towers surrounding us, my new buddies got into a short dispute. They were lost, or at least confused. They argued about which tower was which, apparently not quite as familiar with the area as I was led to believe. In time, we dropped our packs below a mean-looking fist crack splitting a vertical wall. One of them roped up, preparing for the climb.

Rock climbing in Czechoslovakia was certainly different from anywhere I'd ever been before. A lot different. To start, there were those rules, which had been officially codified as laws—and not just ethical suggestions—presumably enforced by police of some sort. At Teplice, there was no modern climbing gear to be seen— no camming devices or nuts—with the official excuse being they could damage the soft sandstone. Thus, climbers used varying diameters of nylon slings and cord with pre-tied overhand knots, makeshift chocks that gave little assurance to the uninitiated that they were worth anything more than psychological protection. Supplementing the knots were the ring bolts. These were big hunks of iron rod with a clipping ring for carabiners, banged into holes drilled into the cliff. While super solid, they were used sparingly and spaced far apart, usually reserved for belay anchors and drilled from the ground-up. This was traditional climbing on steroids.

None of the locals had proper climbing shoes. Instead, they wore what looked like carpet slippers or they climbed barefoot. The slippers didn't look helpful to me, with shiny plastic soles that appeared as slick as Teflon. As for ropes, well, at least they used two of them. They were modern nylon ropes, but heavily worn, likely hand-me-downs acquired from Western climbers. I'd be using my own cord, thank you very much. I figured I could adjust to all these rules and shenanigans save one: I hated that ban on chalk. I'd just have to play by the rules, endure sweaty hands and try not to slip—an unpleasant thought on the poorly protected climbs.

The fist crack wasn't going well. The German on lead, a stout, muscular specimen, was about twenty-five feet off the deck, still with no gear in place. His repeated attempts to jam a knot in the crack had so far only resulted in nylon detritus strewn around the base of the climb, as he tossed each knot to the ground when he couldn't make it work. A little higher, about halfway up the crack to the first huge ring bolt, he started to truly freak out. His yells shifted from anger about not getting any knots to seat to shrieks for help, as he pondered the grim reality of a thirty-foot groundfall. A climber well above him on another route managed to swing over a free end of rope. The German latched it first with one hand and then the other, gripping the strand for dear life as he careened out of the crack and took an impressive pendulum across the wall. The belaying climber then lowered the German back to terra firma, a little scraped up from his skittle along the cliff but otherwise unharmed. What had I gotten myself into? I hoped this wasn't standard fare at the Czechoslovakian crags. If this was normal, I would surely witness a death—if not die myself.

The day was now half shot and, despite watching a climber almost kill himself, I was growing restless. I hadn't even touched rock yet. I asked if they would mind if I tried something. I pointed to a nearby tower with a rounded arête. It was a beautiful line, starting out slightly less than vertical, then steepening with a few bulges before the angle eased near the summit. The arête had a series of horizontal cracks, luring me into thoughts of Gunks-like positive bucket holds and good protection. I could surely get one of those funky knots to stick in a constriction somewhere along the way. Anyway, the climb didn't look too hard.

At the base of the arête, closer inspection revealed three ring bolts protecting the climb, which looked to be about 5.10, with plenty of good rests. The first ring was about thirty feet up, the next at roughly double that distance, and the last around ninety feet up the tower. The Germans consulted their guidebook, found the climb, and showed some concern when they pointed out the grade. However, between the language and climbing-grading-system barriers, we couldn't figure out what the route would be in the Yosemite Decimal System. "It's the most difficult Czech grade," the East Germans told me, whatever that meant. I looked up again at the climb and figured, *Looks around 5.10.*

My progress was immediately stymied while I still had one foot on the ground. The rock down low was holdless, without the slightest edge for either the fingertips or feet, and the first real hold—a horizontal—three feet past my substantial reach. As I tried, and failed, to get going, I heard some laughter nearby and glanced up to see a couple climbers on another route watching my antics. The Germans asked them something, and then they began laughing as well. What the fuck? One German patted his shoulder, signaling me to step on it. Ah, yes. I'd heard that shoulder stands were sometimes used to bypass blank or cruxy spots on the rock, both to get off the ground and at ring-bolt belays.

I stepped onto the crouching German's back and reached the first horizontal, which sloped more than I was hoping and moreover had no constriction to jam a knot. I had to make a scary move, bringing a foot up to my hands, pressing hard with my leg, and balancing upward. This got my hands on the next horizontal, which, again, was sloping and had nowhere to jam a knot. I made another off-balance mantel and stood up, now about twenty feet above the ground.

I wiped my hands on my T-shirt, wishing I had chalk to dry the sweat. I was in no-man's land: marooned above terrain that was too difficult to downclimb, but still with a hard move to make to reach the first bolt. The wall above steepened, and this last horizontal crack I was latching onto before the bolt was the worst yet, even more insecure than the ones below. All chatter had ceased below while everyone stopped to watch me. I put a foot up and started to press, but quickly backed down as my balance wasn't right. More sweating, more hand wiping, and a gradually building pump in my forearms. I had to do something—fast.

I put my foot up and pressed, keeping my hips close to the wall to distribute my weight, rocking over and slowly standing tall. Finally, the ring bolt was in my face, and I was grabbing the first positive, incut holds since leaving the ground. I clipped my rope into that godsent hunk of iron and let go a sigh of relief—until I looked down to see that my "belayer" had let go of the rope and was busy donning his climbing shoes, preparing to climb. My unglued scream bolted him to attention—he'd expected me to climb in the Czech fashion of stopping to belay at each ring bolt, but I made it clear I would attempt to go to the top.

The next section was steeper but had more positive edges—though still no option for jammed-knot protection in the horizontal cracks. The nylon knots hung off my harness gear loops, doing nothing but adding some weight. About ten feet below the second bolt, the rock bulged again and the good edges vanished, leaving me pawing at sloping fingertip holds and relying on friction for my feet. The only consolation was that I might survive a fall if my belayer paid close attention and ran from the base of the wall to take in slack, as they often do on the short, runout gritstone routes in the United Kingdom. Hopefully he was familiar with the drill.

I squeaked through the holdless crux and clipped the second bolt. Above, though the rock lessened in angle, the holds totally ran out, presenting me with twenty feet of nervy and unrelenting friction climbing. I had to carefully search for the slightest irregularity or indentation on the stone for a foothold, and I

Jiri on a typical Czechoslovakian runout, 1984

brushed each foot carefully against my pant leg to remove any sand that may have attached to my sticky-rubber shoes before holding my breath and gently stepping up. Some minutes later, I clipped the last ring bolt and stood on top of the little tower, sweaty and drained but also elated that I'd made it. I took a moment to look around at the surrounding towers sprouting from the pine forest to relax my taxed nerves. Even by Gunks standards for "scary," this thing I'd just done was a new level of fucking frightening.

The next morning dawned cloudy. I did another fruitless check around the campsites for Bob and Beth, thinking, *Where the hell were they?* and then joined my East German partners for another outing. We stuck to easier climbs they knew well, so the day was less hair-raising than the previous one. Since it was a Sunday and my new friends had a long drive back home, they called it quits by midafternoon. I had no idea what to do next, and the Germans knew that. They gave me a ride to a café near the campground, telling me it was often frequented by climbers. The tables on the outdoor terrace were busy, and many in the crowd were indeed climbers, identifiable by their packs and ropes. I got a coffee and sat at a small corner table.

As I stared absentmindedly up at the towers surrounding me, an accented "Hello" came from behind. It was the woman climber who'd been in my cabin on the train ride from Prague. She smiled and beckoned me with a wave to a large table of her friends. Just as I was steeling myself for another frustrating round of nods and sign language, a fellow stood up and said, "Hi, I'm Michael. What's your name?"

Michael was a blessing for me and a rarity in Czechoslovakia then: a language teacher who taught English, not Russian. And, again, luckily for all of us there, also a climber. Michael began a two-hour session as translator. I was introduced to everyone, doing my best to remember their names. Eva and Rodek were the couple from the train. It turned out they had heard about "the American—or was he English?" guy on the arête yesterday. Apparently, I'd gained some notoriety for an early repeat of one of their hardest routes, and now they were anxious to show me around. While honored, I was also wary—being "shown around" here could be hazardous to one's health.

I asked Michael if he knew of any Brits in the area, asking about Bob and Beth. He knew Bob from a previous visit, but had not seen him around, nor had anyone else. The Czechs registered the disappointment on my face. Most of the group lived in Prague and would return to the city for work during the week. But Jiri, who lived locally, had plenty of free time to go climb. He had a few words of English too—just enough to allow us to make climbing plans together. Jiri was psyched to climb with a visitor, especially the rare American. I wasn't sure of his ability at first, but when we got out climbing, I found his skill level was high, as well as his boldness. He was a little younger than me, and his gear, like everyone's here, looked old and worn. Jiri was built much like me, thin and standing around six feet tall, with light-brown hair, his face framed by his glasses and some peachfuzz on his upper lip.

Jiri and I got along so well that I exited the campground, leaving my tent up and paying the daily fee in order to keep getting my visa stamped. I moved into the guest room at his family home, where his parents seemed happy to host me. Their house was close by the campground, a tidy cottage in a cluster of homes on a quiet street. Each night, the family gathered around a large table for dinner—usually some version of cauliflower: baked cauliflower, braised cauliflower, fried cauliflower, boiled cauliflower—and the atmosphere exuded warmth. Rapid chatter flowed easily around the table, completely unintelligible to me, and I never knew who was who exactly, since the diners weren't always the same. The dinner guests peppered me with questions, and Jiri would do his best to translate, but his English skills were more useful with simple climbing jargon than intricate questions about me or my country. Meanwhile, if I devoured my plateful too quickly, Jiri's mother took note and refilled it. Even when I was beyond full, she'd encourage me to eat more, gesturing that I was too skinny. Their hospitality was some of the most generous I'd experienced. It even made me forget my wayward friends, Bob and Beth.

Jiri and I sought out the area's testpieces. He was just as motivated as me to get after it, and under his tutelage, I got better at placing the knotted slings and even took a few falls onto some. Those falls increased my confidence about how much force the knots could hold when properly placed. The crux was learning what was a "good" placement versus what wasn't, and sometimes the difference was very subtle. I was astonished at the difficulty of some of these routes—into the solid 5.12 range, but without the "comforts" we used back home. I'd never give up my rack of nuts and cams—much less modern climbing shoes and chalk—for a handful of knotted slings in the Gunks. And I didn't even want to think of the old ropes Czech climbers were using. It made the climbs back in the States, even the Gunks, where we prided ourselves on our heroic boldness, look like a frolic.

Jiri suggested we should do two "very hard, very good" routes toward the end of my stay. Their names, roughly translated to the best of our abilities, were *Complex Gravity* and *Happy Ending*. *Happy Ending* caught my eye instantly, not just for the beautiful, seemingly blank vertical wall it ascended but also for the abundance of rings—by Czech standards anyway. It was a mere twenty feet or so between the rings, all four of them, making it, by far, the safest-looking climb I'd seen since arriving. However, Jiri insisted we first try *Complex Gravity*, despite my preference. When we got to the tower, it was clear why he'd insisted: the climb was gorgeous, threading its way up an arching crack to a ring bolt, then up a steep face past another ring bolt, one hundred feet to the summit. The day was pure magic; the kind that every climber seeks when it all comes together—the right mental state to go for it and the strength to pull off the moves. We ticked both climbs, sharing the lead and pushing the high point on *Complex Gravity*, and with me flashing *Happy Ending*, lured upward by the "safe," merely twenty-foot runouts.

My trip was coming to a speedy conclusion. It was almost mid-September, and my flight out of Frankfort was about ten days off, leaving me time to sneak in some more climbing en route to the airport. I felt a sadness about leaving this friendly crew, knowing full well there was little chance I'd ever see any of them again. It wasn't easy, or in many cases, possible, for residents of Soviet-controlled Eastern Europe to visit the West. As for a future visit for myself, I wasn't sure I wanted to chance it. I truly felt fortunate to be leaving without injury. I insisted on taking my new climbing buddies out to celebrate on my last night in Teplice. At the climber bar, we took up the largest table. I did my best to repay my hosts' hospitality by springing for all the food they could eat and beer they could drink, but even so I barely put a dent in my funds. Pilsner, for example, only cost the equivalent of ten cents a liter.

The train to Prague left at 3:00 a.m. the next day after our celebratory dinner. During the ride back, I reflected on my luck. A couple of weeks earlier, I would have considered the prospect of not finding Bob and Beth dreadful. But it had in fact been a great bit of luck, one that let me experience the Czech climbing scene firsthand, meet a wonderful band of climbers, and get an inside tour of the towers. It had been the kind of experience that only a climber might have, showing up in a foreign country, solo and not speaking the language, but within mere hours being plugged into the local scene, all through the lingua franca that is rock climbing. And as for the missing Beth and Bob? Well, I didn't have their address or phone number back in England, neglecting to get those details when we were at the pub in Sheffield making our plans. I had no easy way to contact them to find out what had happened. In fact, the last time I ever saw them was over those beers.

On one of my early trips to Yosemite Valley, I had been fooling around in the makeshift Camp 4 gym, which was housed in the Yosemite Search and Rescue squad's tent area. There were various workout contraptions, including pullup bars and a long rope ladder strung between two trees at a steep angle. This invention was the Bachar Ladder, originally conceived by a leading climber of the era, John Bachar. The concept was that you'd grab a rung, do an assisted one-arm pullup pushing with the lower arm and pulling with the lead one, and then grab the next rung at the apex of this locked-off position. It was a brutal workout—one that left more than a few climbers with elbow tendonitis—and not without consequences of an injurious tumble as one got higher on the ladder if you lost all strength.

That day, I was joined by a heavily muscled guy with a shag of dark shoulder-length hair. I recognized him immediately: it was

Wolfgang Güllich, a well-known young star of the West German climbing scene. He was often photographed in the climbing mags, climbing the world's hardest routes; it was Wolfgang's modus operandi. He'd travel to a climbing area with an agenda to repeat the hardest climbs there and then do so, as well as establish with frightening regularity the toughest climbs at his home area, the Frankenjura. While we were in that ersatz gym in Camp 4, I could see why he succeeded on his quests. Wolf would go on to establish the world's first 5.14a (*Punks in the Gym*, at Mount Arapiles), 5.14b (*Wall Street*, in the Frankenjura), and 5.14d sport climbs (*Action Directe*, also in the Frankenjura).

Wolfgang was stronger than any climber I'd ever seen. He used the Bachar Ladder with ease, his biceps looking like grapefruits as he pumped up and down the contraption. He gave off a friendly vibe, and we chatted between sets of pullups. Wolf told me he had been to the Gunks and had climbed the hard routes there, including *Supercrack*. We didn't climb together that trip, and though our hang was brief, I immediately liked the guy.

So, while my train chugged through West Germany from Czechoslovakia, I decided to climb my last days of the trip in the Frankenjura. The Frankenjura, with its hundreds of limestone outcrops spread over a vast region of forest and small villages, had become the hands-down center ring for the new sport climbing game. Since the last time I'd been in West Germany, three years ago, sport climbing had taken full control of the scene. No longer did people pull on pitons, or even place them. They'd switched over instead to the much safer expansion bolts, and the degree of difficulty soared. The routes generally were not long—mostly fifty to seventy feet—but they tended to be technical and powerful, with lots of small pockets and edges.

When the train pulled into Nuremburg, I was now in the middle of the West German climbing universe, but I had nobody to climb with plus no idea where the actual cliffs were. I found my way to a local outdoor store, where an affable employee greeted me. He was another climber I'd read about in the magazines. Flipper Fietz was a powerful boulderer, way before bouldering was a mainstream aspect of climbing. He did extremely hard moves at the base of cliffs, climbing the first fifteen or twenty feet before dropping off. Eventually, many of those starts became routes that went higher, but Flipper didn't care about that. When I asked if he was free to do some climbing, Flipper said he was working during the week and didn't have time to show me around.

"But you must know Wolfgang, no?" he asked.

I said I'd met him in Yosemite a couple years back, but really didn't know him that well. Also, since that brief meeting, Wolfgang had just gotten better and better, and I found the idea of climbing with him a little unnerving. However, before I could say anything more, Flipper rang up Wolfgang. After a short conversation in German, Flipper handed the phone to me.

"Wolfgang?" I asked.

"Yes," he replied, in his Teutonic baritone.

"This is Russ Clune. We met in the Valley a couple years ago, at Camp 4."

"Yes," he said again, before an awkward pause ensued as I waited for more. I wondered if he remembered me—or if reaching out to him to climb was even a good idea.

"Yeah, well, I'm in the area for the next week or so," I explained hurriedly, "and I'm wondering if you have time to do some climbing?"

Again, a moment of hesitation, followed by Wolfgang's response: "I'll pick you up in ten minutes." With that, the line went dead. I handed the phone back to Flipper.

Wolfgang got to the shop in ten minutes, as promised. He greeted Flipper and me with handshakes and the friendly smile I remembered from Yosemite. We jetted down the road to a popular cliff, the Weissenstein. Like many Frankenjura crags, the limestone block was steep, compact, short at only about fifty feet in height, and riddled with pockets of various sizes. A group of climbers was there, some on their routes, others sitting on the flat, grassy area at the base.

Wolfgang introduced me to Andreas Kubin, the editor of *Der*

Wolfgang's kitchen table: L to R: Wolfgang, Ron Fawcett, Clune, unknown, Tomas Düll

Bergstieger, a magazine that featured climbing and mountaineering topics; Andreas' girlfriend, Andrea; and some other friends. Much to my delight, Ron Fawcett, the English legend, and his wife, Jill, were also there. I'd not seen them for a few years, and it turned out they were staying at Wolfgang's house, where Wolf had invited me to stay as well. I asked which route I should warm up. Wolf pointed out *Dampfhammer*, a classic "VIII" in the European UIAA grading system, which I translated to about 5.11. It would be a stout warmup, but doable, I figured. The route quickly went from pretty cruiser on a slightly more than vertical wall to a desperate race against the "pump clock." My arms tired quickly, telling me I was not properly warmed up and that my fingers would soon give out. The wall steepened abruptly, the pockets grew smaller and I lost round one as the rock spat me off, blowing my forearms up into tight balloons. I expected to just be lowered to the ground, but instead was held fast when my short fall stopped. *Oh yeah, I'm in the sport-climbing world now*, I realized. I got back on the rock to sort out the moves. The difference from Czechoslovakia was shocking; I could lob off a climb and not potentially die.

While I rested, Andreas came over, congratulating me on the effort. Apparently, he liked a good fight, regardless of the outcome. We talked about the Gunks, the places I'd been on my European trip, and the like. He noticed a book I had in my pack, one I'd picked up in England before my long train ride to Czechoslovakia called *Schindler's Ark*, and asked what it was about. I felt my face flush red, recalling the time in the Rhineland Pfalz with Melinda a few years earlier when I'd innocently asked an older German if he'd ever been to England before and he replied he had—as a P.O.W. in World War II. There was no easy way to avoid the awkwardness, so I just spit it out: "Well, it's a story about the war and a man who tried to save Jews by having them work in his factory." Andreas gave me a serious look and took a long pull on his cigarette. "Not the most pleasant time in our history, I'm afraid," he said.

Wolfgang lived in a lovely little house on a quiet street, Moselstrasse, in the suburb of Obershollenbach, a short distance northeast of Nuremburg. Like all the homes in the area, it was tidy, with a small yard and garden. He shared the house with his good friend and regular climbing partner, Kurt Albert, along with Ingrid Reitenspiess and Norbert Sandner. Norbert lived on the top floor of the house, in a small, separate apartment. Kurt was a bit older than Wolfgang and to a degree, had been his mentor. He was another amazingly muscular specimen, much like Wolfgang, but taller, with a tangled mop of curly, light-brown hair framing a mustache as thick as a wooly caterpillar.

Wolf led me down a narrow set of stairs to my sleeping quarters, a small stack of foam pads in the basement. The basement was a perfect nest—cool, dark, and quiet, a nice reprieve from the upstairs kitchen, where the often-raucous social gatherings occurred. Mornings at the house started gradually, and always with a large pot of strong coffee. Somebody would make a run to the local bakery and return with assorted breads and pastries. As we stuffed our faces and got jacked up on caffeine, I soaked up all the local lore, including how sport climbing had taken off in Western Europe over the past couple of years.

The war between the old guard and the new generation had come to an end, with the young climbers the hands-down victors. No longer was it acceptable to grab gear to climb past difficult moves—to "French-free" the routes, as it had come to be called. Instead, the American and British concept of what constituted a "free" ascent was the same on the continent now, but with a major twist: It was now fair game to place bolts on rappel, with a power drill if you so desired. Along with that, a new concept of what made for a "proper" ascent emerged with the "redpoint," a practice championed by Kurt Albert.

The redpoint—or rotpunkt in German—idea was simple enough: When a climber successfully free-climbed a route on lead for the first time, they painted a red circle at the base to indicate that any points of aid had been eliminated and the route was now a free climb. These climbs were often done in yo-yo style, much like the accepted style in the United States: If the leader fell, they could leave the rope attached to their high point and start again from the ground on toprope. Once a climber had led the route from the ground up, placing all the gear on that attempt and not taking any falls, the route was now "redpointed" and the "red circle" was filled in to show the new status. The idea caught fire, and now hundreds of climbs had red dots at their bases.

The new approach had nothing to do with the old rules; redpointing allowed the climber to work out all the moves, hanging on the rope indiscriminately to figure out the most efficient way to make progress. It was a utilitarian style that set aside all discussions of fair play and put the focus on the final result—like an Olympic gymnast perfecting her floor routine, the top climbers could now "dial in" the hardest routes, with the ultimate goal of linking them in one, continuous sequence from bottom to top, no matter how long it took to get there. These new sport-climbing/redpointing "rules" led to an explosion of difficult routes in Europe, especially France and West Germany. Kurt's *Magnet* is a fine example. He knocked this testpiece out in 1982, and Wolfgang did the second ascent soon after. *Magnet* was given IX+ on the UIAA scale, or 5.13b on the US system. Wolfgang upped the ante significantly in 1984 with his *Kanal im Rucken*, rated UIAA X, or 5.13d, then the single hardest free climb in the world. Meanwhile, in France, Buoux became a hotbed of progression. Once those walls were bolted up, the pocket-pulling began in earnest. Marc Le Menestrel's *Reve de Papillon* ushered in the French grade of 8a (5.13b) in 1983, then Marc's brother, Antoine, bested his sibling's effort on Buoux's Bout du Monde wall with *Chouca* in 1984, weighing in at 8a+ (5.13c), a harbinger of even harder things to come quite soon. Meanwhile, US climbers, still adhering to traditional ethics, began to fall far behind. The hardest route in America remained Tony Yaniro's *Grand Illusion*, done in 1979, at a solid 5.13. As great as Yaniro's achievement was at that time, nothing had been done to surpass it in all those years, essentially because of the old trad mindset. The only exception to the old ways was up at that backwater, central Oregon crag I'd visited in the summer of '82. Alan Watts was transforming Smith Rock into a sport climbing haven, and Smith was well on its way to becoming the place for pushing the grades in the US.

I asked Kurt where the idea for the redpoint marking came from. I mean, why a "redpoint"? Why not a "blackpoint," or a "greenpoint"? He motioned to the coffee pot we drank from every morning. There was a large red spot on the lip of the pot. In order to pour coffee, one had to align the spot to the lip of the spout. Ahh, now that made sense! There was no climbing without coffee in the Moselstrasse house!

I was excited by what I saw in West Germany. I told myself "Fuck it" and left my trad brain behind, embracing the new style while I was there. To have done otherwise would have made me look downright stupid to the local climbers. And just like I'd experienced in 1981 with my first taste of sport climbing, I did some hard routes quickly after hangdogging and rehearsal. The sport-climbing mentality had made its argument, and it made sense. If the intent of rock climbing was to climb ever-more difficult routes, the Europeans had proven their point. The traditional climbing tactics used in the States were archaic, like bringing knives to a gun fight, or maybe more like throwing stones in a nuclear war. But the question for many traditional climbers was, if pure physical difficulty was the only point, then what would become of boldness? Would there still be routes that were psychological testpieces, with long runouts into the unknown above self-placed gear? And would the rock still have a chance to "win," by dint of climbers not knowing what lay above them on a ground-up lead?

I didn't have my own answer to those questions yet, so I decided to have my cake and eat it too. I would adhere to the traditional climbing methods while back home in the Gunks, at least for now, splitting my tendencies depending on where I was climbing and doing the old, "When in Rome" thing. I surely wouldn't use a traditional mindset anymore in a sport-climbing area, but I was also hesitant to go full-bore and start rap-bolting and creating havoc in my own sandbox.

GAMSAHABNIDA! KIMCHI AND CRACK CLIMBS

"People will forget what you said, forget what you did, but people will never forget how you made them feel."

—Maya Angelou

I wrote an article about Gunks climbing for the Japanese magazine *Iwa to Yuki,* which resulted in an invitation to visit Japan to climb in early 1985. As long as I was going that far, I wanted to see what South Korea had to offer as well. A climbing buddy from the Gunks had been stationed in the country while in the Army and said there were good granite domes just outside Seoul. He connected me to his friends there, and they agreed to take me on a tour of Korean rock.

My two weeks in Japan were blissful. I spent most of my time on the seaside cliffs of Jogasaki, with incredible hosts and fun crack climbing on the columnar basalt, savoring the best that climbing travel has to offer: hanging out with other like-minded souls who are happy to be outdoors and trying our hardest on the rock. I began to regret my plans for South Korea, especially when a couple of the Japanese climbers told me the rock there was mostly low-angle slabs and the weather would be miserable in early March.

My contact in Korea, Cho Sang Hee, picked me up at the Seoul airport. He wore a suit and tie and in no way resembled a climber. He worked at an English-language newspaper, so communication was simple. He explained to me that while he no longer climbed himself, he remained good friends with his old partners and could plug me in. South Korea had a very active mountaineering community, but rock climbing for the pursuit of difficulty and its own rewards wasn't a game much played. The Koreans climbed on the big granite domes just outside the city, Insu Bong and Sunin Bong, principally for alpine practice, pulling on their gear with abandon and moving as quickly as possible, since in the mountains, as the adage goes, "speed is safety." South Korean climbing was also hyper-organized. If you wanted to climb, you joined a club. From there, you learned the basics. Any novice climber became the low man on the totem pole during club outings, which meant, as a peon, you did a lot of cooking, cleaning, and errand running for the older members until you graduated up the ladder.

Cho took me to a local climbing shop called Half Dome, where a bunch of his old partners worked and gathered. While everyone there was quite friendly, they didn't really know what to make of me and my nonexistent mountaineering and alpine climbing résumé—it seemed that tagging high points along the Appalachian Trail didn't count for much. I explained what I had come over for: big granite domes with lots of possibilities for new routes. They arranged for me to meet up with a club member the next morning at my hotel. I would be accompanied by Lee, the club's unfortunate low-man workhorse. Lee would oversee taking the lanky American up to the club hut on Insu Bong.

Clune on FFA, "Butternuts," 5.11, South Korea, 1985

Lee arrived early to the hotel to fetch me. Outside, a cold wind stung my face and clouds scuttled across the sky, with only a few rays of sun breaking through. Lee didn't speak English, but we managed effective enough communication with gestures, his few English words, and my only Korean one: "*gamsahabnida*" (thank you). A short bus ride from downtown Seoul deposited us at the trailhead, where we found the hillside covered in snow and the steep trail packed with ice. The massive hulk of Insu Bong looming above was impressive, but it was so freezing and unpleasant here that I had a hard time imagining climbing.

The next morning, the temperature was well below freezing and it was breezy. Lee and I had done a little cragging on a short cliff above the hut the afternoon before, and both of our hands had gone numb in the cold. I was pretty sure climbing would not be happening today, and contentedly sat by the stove sipping tea. Around 10:30, the door flung open and a large entourage entered. My initial contact, Cho, had arrived with a slew of his old club-mates plus a few people from the South Korean climbing magazine. Cho introduced me to the group and my climbing partner for the day, Yoon Dae-Pyo. Yoon was short, with broad shoulders and a trim waist. His English was limited, which didn't matter since he didn't speak to me much. I wondered if he'd been bamboozled into this fiasco, to come climb with some random American dude with zero alpine credentials. In contrast, Yoon was a Korean climbing celebrity; he'd done many routes in the Himalayas and the Alps, most of them firsts for a South Korean. From his standoffish attitude, I guessed he felt like an NBA star who'd been talked into a pickup game on a street corner. Our route that day, I was told, would be the classic *Skyline/Dragon* linkup, which, I would unfortunately learn, was on the shady side of the dome.

While a small party of photographers started up an adjacent route to document our climb, Yoon uncoiled the rope at the base of the first pitch, a diagonal crack cutting up a slab. He hadn't yet smiled at me nor offered a word. I didn't know if he was pissed off or just all business, so I didn't try to make small talk. Yoon tied in, racked up, and handed me the belay end of the cord. With a stone-faced look, he barked, "I guide!" and then sprinted off up the fissure, placing very little gear. The rope came tight on me, and I started up the pitch, climbing it slowly, stopping to blow warm air into my numb hands every few moves. As soon as I stepped onto the belay ledge, Yoon demanded, "How hard?" I wasn't too sure, since my hands hadn't felt a damn thing since leaving the ground. I replied, "Maybe 5.7 or 5.8?" Yoon grunted and gave a nod. He put his hand out, signaling he wanted me to pass over the gear. He re-racked the gear on his harness, once again said, "I guide!" and once again sprinted off up the rock. The same brusque interview took place after pitch two: "How hard?" Yoon asked. "Maybe 5.9?" I replied, as Yoon snatched the gear from me to lead the next pitch.

At the end of the crack system, we arrived at a wide slab tilted at 80 degrees. A bolt ladder stretched above the belay, with pieces of old webbing hanging from many of the bolt hangers. The wind had died, and the sun now crept onto the cliff, warming me, while Yoon climbed a few feet up to the first bolt. He pulled up on it, and then did so again with the remainder of the closely spaced bolts. At the final one, Yoon shouted something I didn't understand, but I eventually realized he wanted me to take the rope tight so he could tension-traverse leftward to the belay. I fed slack slowly, lowering him slightly as he swung over to the ledge.

I looked up at the slab; it looked doable as a free climb, dotted with just enough small edges and crystals to allow passage. I decided to give it a shot. The rock was solid and coarse, biting nicely into my soles and luring me up to the top of the traverse. I unclipped the last bolt and considered my position. There was now no gear between me and Yoon, who was twenty feet to my left and slightly lower. If I fell, I'd take a horrendous, forty-plus-foot pendulum. I slowed down and climbed carefully. When I arrived at the belay, Yoon's eyes were wide, and he gently shook his head. "How hard?!" he asked. For the first time, it sounded like an honest inquiry, not an inquisitor's demand. "Probably 5.11," I answered. Yoon smiled, handed me the rack, and said, "YOU GUIDE!" I laughed, clapped him on the shoulder, and started up the next pitch, this time on the sharp end.

Next on the climbing agenda was Seoul's other big dome, Sunin Bong, where Lee and I arrived the day after the outing to Insu Bong. I was feeling somewhat the worse for wear after a club dinner the previous evening that had involved too much Soju, the local firewater. We were to meet Yoon at the trailhead in the early afternoon. He'd been sold on the idea of free-climbing after our outing on the *Skyline/Dragon* route, and was anxious to show me some promising lines he thought would go free. Along our hike to the crag, we came to a forty-foot boulder split by an overhanging finger crack. I stopped in my tracks; it was gorgeous. The crack was fifteen degrees beyond vertical and filled with pitons left behind by climbers practicing their aid technique. I said I wanted to try freeing the climb.

As soon as I did the opening moves, I knew I was in for a battle. The crack was way harder than it looked, and the fixed pitons impeded many of the best fingerlocks. I borrowed a piton hammer from Yoon and went around to the top to drop a rope. I hammered away for twenty minutes, removing most of the pins, leaving a few for protection for a lead attempt. But first I wanted to work the route on toprope.

Most of the finger jams were insecure in the flaring crack, and there was nothing for the feet aside from the thin crack itself. At first, I couldn't link the moves together, many requiring me to move dynamically between jams, almost lunging from one to the next. I was essentially doing a series of one-armed pull-ups. With my fingers swollen and bleeding after a series of tries, we left the crack and continued up the hill. Lee set up a large dome tent at our campsite near the base of the cliffs. Since Koreans worked Monday through Saturday, we were on our own until Sunday, when the crowds would arrive for their one day of recreation. When they did come, it appeared all of Seoul emptied out onto the hillsides. But during the week, the place was all ours. The weather improved, too. The cold front gave way to warmer temperatures and the sun finally had a spring warmth to it.

On our first full day on Sunin Bong, Yoon led Lee and I to an objective he had in mind, an immaculate white wall of vertical granite with a splitter finger crack soaring straight up it for seventy-five feet to a ledge. Above, a second pitch climbed a large roof and corner system with a hand crack running along its fifteen-foot underside. If these pitches were in Yosemite, they'd be two of the Valley's most sought-after classics, but here in Korea, nobody had even attempted to free-climb them. Yoon looked at my wide-eyed expression and laughed. I think he was as happy as me and I couldn't get my shoes on fast enough. A more perfect 5.11 finger crack didn't exist anywhere. The second pitch was just as beautiful but more physical. The roof had poor footholds but the hand jams in the crack were solid for me, and

Korean hosts and partners

gave another splendid pitch of 5.11. I no longer questioned the wisdom of my trip here, and over the next week and a half, Yoon presented me with the first free ascents of some of the best crack climbs I'd done anywhere. Each morning over breakfast, Yoon would declare, "Now a 5.13 climb for you!"—though most of these routes ended up being 5.11 or 5.12.

I also returned to that finger crack in the boulder several times, and eventually toproped it cleanly. It was desperate, beating the shit out of my fingers each time I attempted it. I never had time to try it on lead, but I was happy enough to get up the thing, even if only on a toprope. I left Yoon with a 5.13 after all.

My trip ended too soon, and before I knew it, I was on my way back to New York. The South Koreans had treated me generously and thanked me for showing them what modern rock climbing looked like. *Thank* me*?!* They'd given me the biggest gift any rock climber could ask for: two weeks of first free ascents on excellent granite. Thanking me was like having Walt Disney thank you for attending his park after letting you in for free and emptying the place of all other visitors. As much as anything else, the warmth and friendliness the Korean community had showered me with was the epitome of the tribal good vibe of the rock-climbing scene that I lived for.

About six months later, I received a letter from Yoon. He had dedicated himself to repeating some of the routes I'd done and was having a great time as a reformed mountaineer-turned-rock-climber. He gave me the blow-by-blow of his successes and attempts, and I was impressed by his rapid progress. About five years after my trip, while climbing in Red Rocks, Las Vegas, I was introduced to a South Korean climber. When he heard my name, his ears perked up. He said my trip had changed Korean climbing. According to him, the Korean climbing magazine put out a reward for the first person who could repeat all the routes I'd done. Within a year, they had all been repeated, except one. That short crack, now known as *Nemesis Crack*, repelled its suitors for just a little while longer.

STORMING THE CASTLE AND EVERYTHING GOES SIDEWAYS

I was early to finish, I was late to start

I might be an adult, I'm a minor at heart

Go to college, be a man, what's the fucking deal?

It's not how old I am, it's how old I feel

—Minor Threat

Wolfgang Güllich and I climbed together for the spring and summer of 1985, including a stint at Elbsandsteingebirge, near Dresden, East Germany. It was a place I'd long wanted to visit, with many similarities, including the "rules," to the sandstone towers of Czechoslovakia where I'd climbed the year before, and equally steeped in climbing lore. Germans had been climbing there since the mid-nineteenth century, and the standard was high even without modern protection. As an example, the first US 5.11s showed up in the 1960s, and that was with reliable nylon ropes, solid pitons for protection, and decent (for the day) footwear. Taking a lead fall while pushing difficulty was unlikely to result in an emergency room visit. In Dresden, however, the best climbers were already about a decade ahead of the States for that level of difficulty. Herbert Richter produced *Fledermausweg* in 1958; at 5.11, it was certainly one of the hardest free climbs around back then, if not *the* most difficult. Topping it off, the Dresden climbers did their ballsy climbs using ropes not much better than clotheslines, pieces of knotted string jammed into crevices for protection, and while climbing barefoot. All that on climbs where a lead fall could easily mean death. The level of danger bordered on suicidal.

When I arrived at Wolf's place in Obershollenbach in May, he'd just returned from a long trip to Australia. Wolfgang had used that vacation time well, establishing the futuristic overhanging-crimp climb, *Punks in the Gym*, at Arapiles. I knew the route—I'd climbed part of it on my trip in 1983, a 5.12 version called *Punks in the Gunks* that veered off the plumb line, escaping to easier climbing and avoiding the obvious headwall above, which yielded the world's first 5.14a.

We packed up Wolf's minivan with the gear we needed for East Germany: a new rope and lots of nylon slings in various sizes, their ends tied in overhand knots. Most importantly, we bought lots of coffee and chocolate for our host, Bernd Arnold, and his family. Good coffee and chocolate were in short supply and very expensive in East Germany.

As we crossed the "Iron Curtain," the smooth asphalt of the autobahn turned into a jostling mixture of cobblestones and patchwork tarmac, but the countryside was beautiful, with fields of yellow flowers and green meadows melting into dark evergreen forests. As the sun lowered into the evening sky, we came into Dresden, a depressing city of gray, still showing the scars of a war forty years gone. Beyond the city, small roads led into the woods. I caught my first glimpse of the fabled towers, and my heart jumped at the size of them. They were big, dark, steep, and scary looking in the twilight.

In the mid-1970s, one of the leading American climbers, Henry Barber—a member of the Gunks' Gang of Four from the early 1970s—made a trip to Dresden and wrote an article about the climbing. Barber was known for his hard solos and ability to keep his shit together in scary situations, and the area suited his skills perfectly. During his visit, he was awed by the high standard of climbing on the East German towers, and especially by the top climber in the area then, Bernd Arnold. Bernd had authored the hardest routes, pushing local standards to the equivalent of hard 5.12 in the Yosemite Decimal System, and was still doing so at the time of my visit. At the Arnold household in Hohnstein, just a short drive from the plethora of towers, Bernd and Wolfgang exchanged friendly greetings. Wolf introduced me to Bernd; his wife, Christine; and daughter, Heike. None of them spoke English, but they were obviously happy to see us—and the chocolate and coffee as well.

Bernd was in his mid-thirties then, but he looked younger. His shock of curly brown hair lacked any hint of gray, which surprised me, considering how many dangerous, horror-show routes he'd put up in his life. He was trim and fit, with the physique of someone who'd committed his life to his climbing passion. Wolfgang translated a few questions and replies for Bernd and me before suggesting we go grab some dinner. He explained in the car that it wouldn't be polite to eat at their house, since it was an expense for them that wasn't easily absorbed. We went to a local hotel to grab a bite. While we ate, I pulled a folded piece of paper from my pocket. It was a list I'd put together of routes from Barber's article. Wolf looked up from his plate.

"What is that?" he asked. I passed over the list. Wolf gave it a cursory look, and then shook his head.

"Forget these climbs," he declared. "They are old routes, not very hard, but dangerous. There's no need to risk your life on easy climbs!"

Wolfgang explained his logic: the more modern routes, though hardly what anyone would consider "well-protected," usually had more of those big ring bolts, since they tackled faces that were devoid of cracks. So, by going for these, we'd spend less time trying to jam potentially useless knots into cracks and more time doing hard moves in relative safety. Never mind that, on some of these climbs, the first ring bolt was forty feet up. This was Wolf's twelfth trip to the area, so there was no sense in arguing. Besides, he had his own agenda. Each time Wolfgang visited Dresden, it was to repeat the hardest routes put up since his previous stay. He had his own lengthy list, and that would be the one we would adhere to.

The East German climbers traditionally used each ring bolt as a belay station, but often on these newer climbs, these belays were not natural stances where a climber could take his hands off—they were simply stopping points where the climber had been able to pause, hanging off a flimsy jammed knot in a small seam or a sling over a flake of rock, and drill. Wolfgang and I set out to "properly" free-climb these newest routes in redpoint, or at least "yo-yo" style, and eliminate the hanging belays. That led to some fantastically long plummets. Sometimes we succeeded in freeing a climb by our own stated rules, but other times, not so much. We had climbs where we found ourselves suddenly facing a blank section of wall, nary a ripple to grab, and staring at a ring bolt some three or four feet above. The choice was lunge for the ring or fall. We did both, and when we missed grabbing the bolt, the falls were heart-stopping, with some passing the sixty-foot mark. We never knew what we'd get, since all the routes carried the same grade as defined by the East German system. We also soiled our T-shirts black by constantly wiping sweat from our hands, wishing we could use chalk. It was a constant battle against gravity and fear.

A couple of Bernd's routes were true classics, and I will never forget *Balance of Soul*. This route followed a gorgeous, dead-vertical corner, its two walls as smooth as a mirror. On the right wall was a bolt, about twenty-five feet off the ground. From there, another twenty-five feet of climbing led to the second bolt, this one on the left side of the corner, with no crack in between for knotted protection. Wolfgang put in the first lead effort, climbing to the first bolt before slipping off the slick stemming just above. He had me lower him, untied, and handed the rope to me, saying, "I'll rest a bit. See what you think of the moves above that bolt."

I struggled through the moves to the first bolt, grateful for the hard-earned, yo-yo–style toprope we'd left clipped. I looked up at the distant second bolt and felt a little queasy. The rock was as smooth as a baby's ass, but here and there I detected slight changes in the angle, places where a foot could stick and where I could place a palm in counter-pressure against the opposite wall. It reminded me of a few similar climbs I'd done on granite corner systems, in which technique, balance, and slow, thoughtful movement trumped strength. I lost myself in the moment as I moved higher, right up until I saw that second bolt just above me. I lost my focus and rushed a movement, sending my foot skittering off the wall. Seeing me take to the air, Wolf sprinted down the hillside, sucking in just enough slack to keep me from decking from fifty feet. I hung there, shaking, just two feet off the ground.

"You'll get it next time," Wolf said matter-of-factly, espousing a confidence in my abilities I certainly did not share.

I'd just taken the worst fall of my life, shocked I hadn't hit the deck and maybe killed myself. Yeah, Wolf's fast-twitch reflexes had saved my ass, but really, I wanted to say, "Fuck you—YOU go get it this time!" or untie and go find a beer, or quit climbing altogether. Instead I took a few deep breaths, looked back at Wolf, and started up again. The first moves flowed well, no doubt thanks to the ample adrenaline coursing through my system. I climbed smoothly above the first bolt, ultra-focused on every move, on every rugosity in the rock. I was floating, moving without effort, until Wolf's shouting brought me out of my trance.

"Russ! Clip the bolt! Clip the bolt!"

I was deep in the flow state, focused entirely on each tiny movement, and had almost climbed past the second bolt, which was already at my waist. I quickly clipped it and continued up easier ground to the end of the pitch.

We continued to make our way through Wolfgang's list of routes, but Bernd took us off task by presenting us with a gift. He had prepared a new route that he hadn't climbed to the top of yet, and he wanted to do the first ascent with me, Wolfgang, and another well-known West German climber, Sepp Gschwendtner. The tower was spectacular, rising two hundred vertiginous feet to a small pedestal of a summit.

We each led one pitch of the route, which was equipped with three bolts, and set a belay at each of them, going with the usual Dresden tactics. Between those belay bolts, we relied on whatever knots we could jam into small cracks. We moved like a train up the wall, crowding each other at the belays but having a great time. The Germans insisted I take the final pitch, to be the first member of the team on top. It was an honor I still grin about. The team ascent went smoothly on *White Dove*, with minimal falls, and produced a lovely climb. It was a very special occasion to establish a new route with this trifecta of German legends.

On our last day at the Elbsandstein, Wolfgang still had one route left on his list. The striking arête of *Ice Time* had caught our eye many times during our stay, but since it was supposed to be the hardest one at somewhere in the high 5.12 range or even tougher, we'd left it until now. I took the first pitch, a 5.11 face sprinkled with small edges but with no protection for forty feet, until the first ring bolt, where I had a small, comfortable stance. We knew the climbing got a lot harder from here. The next bolt was about twenty feet above me, the third bolt barely visible high above that one. Beyond that was anyone's guess. I clipped into the first bolt and belayed Wolfgang up.

Bernd had supplied us with a special knotted sling, one he'd used to protect the hard moves above the second bolt. Wolf set off, the knot at the ready, clipped on his harness. About fifteen feet above the second bolt was a small, flaring crack—the placement for the special knot. Wolfgang shoved it in, mashing it with a nut tool and giving it a few tugs to set it. Now with that knot well below his feet, Wolfgang came to a crux move and stalled. His foot skidded off a bad foothold as he tried to mantel upwards, and then off he went, flying down the face, stripping the knot from the crack and taking a fifty-foot fall onto the second bolt.

"That knot is not so good," Wolf said flatly. He went back up for another attempt, again placing the knot, and pulled off a carbon copy of the first fall.

"Fuck this piece-of-shit knot!" Wolf grumbled. He went up for another try, this time leaving the worthless knot behind, and took his third screamer. After that one, he joined me at the belay bolt and clipped in. I laughed at Wolf's mini-fit—at how pissed off he was at the crap knot, the long, but so far safe falls, and the intractability of the moves above. We had been on a good roll, but day after day of doing runout, scary routes had ground us down to nubs, both physically and mentally, and Wolfgang did not appreciate my chuckling.

"Your turn!" he said with a smirk, and then slumped onto the anchor. Suddenly the situation wasn't all that funny.

We swapped ends of the rope, and I made my way up to Wolf's high point. I didn't bother with the knot, deciding to just save my energy for the moves. I tried Wolf's method with the mantel, lost my balance, and took the whipper. Wolfgang shot me a smile and laugh when I stopped falling. "Not so easy!" he said.

I went back up and tried again, spotting two shallow finger pockets out left that we hadn't grabbed yet. The holds looked promising, but they also meant a bigger fall, and as I pressed up onto a sloping foothold, some grains of sand rolled under my sole and I fell again—even farther this time, taking more of a swing.

"That was a good one!" Wolf said with a laugh.

We swapped ends once more, with Wolfgang mastering the move this time and continuing to the top of the tower. Once beyond that troublesome move, the climbing stayed difficult but nothing came up as hard as the bit lower down. We'd finished

Ice Time, but not before our rope sustained hundreds of feet of terrifying falls.

Wolfgang's next-door neighbors were a group of young people sharing a house. Some of the tenants were climbers, and they came over most evenings to Wolf's to sit around the kitchen table and socialize. One of them, Gabi, was a slim and athletic woman, with soft brown eyes and short light-brown hair. She had an easy smile and laughed at the jokes we told. We had plenty of stories from our East Germany trip, but one of Gabi's favorites was about our exit from the country. At the border, the guards had questioned Wolfgang for a long while, the exchange heating up until he'd burst out laughing. I'd asked what the problem was. Wolf looked at me, still wearing my fluorescent-green leopard-print Lycra tights, and said, "They don't believe you are a climber! They say no climber wears pants like that!" The guards only relented once we showed them our climbing gear.

Gabi joined us for climbing on her days off from work, and I soon found myself upgrading from Wolfgang's basement to her substantially more comfortable bedroom.

Gabi was a great companion. She was a good climber, a patient belayer, and helped me chill out about my projects. She made a day spent flailing on a route seem less like a failure and more like a stepping stone toward success. Her presence was calming, and our conversations during rests between burns ranged across topics far from climbing. I loved climbing with Wolfgang, but Gabi was a pleasant break from my usual routine, especially after the mentally taxing routes in East Germany.

One morning over breakfast, Wolfgang asked me if I would be interested in going to Italy for a climbing competition—in fact, what was going to be the first-ever professional competition—held on the limestone walls near the ski town of Bardonecchia. Wolfgang had talked to the Sportroccia organizers and explained I was climbing with him for the summer, and should be invited. But even with our invitations, Wolfgang and I were on the fence about going, not sure what to expect.

Climbing competitions were nothing new, but to date they'd been strictly casual, amateur affairs. In the States, they usually took place at bouldering areas, and were grassroots events with some swag prizes. There were also international meets, during which one country's alpine club would arrange with another's to have some of the best climbers from each country challenge themselves on routes in the host country, or in speed competitions on long mountain routes. These gatherings were competitive in a friendly way, and were held to build camaraderie between national climbing organizations. Wolfgang and I figured Bardonecchia would be of this same ilk, even though prize money was involved. We made the trip into a mini-vacation, with Gabi joining us, along with an American friend of mine from the Gunks, Frank Minunni. Frank was on his first trip overseas, having met Wolfgang the previous fall at the Gunks.

When we arrived at the competition site, we were amazed at the size of the production. It took place in Valle Stretta, a stunning mountain valley high above town. Large sponsor tents had been pitched along the hillside, and cars from all over Europe packed the parking area. We'd never seen anything like it in the climbing world. Meanwhile, the competition routes had been manufactured up blank panels in the limestone, the setters chipping edges, gluing on holds, and in some cases filling in rest stances with cement to create the desired level of difficulty. I was aghast at the blatant breach of protocol: as a rule, climbers avoid chipping, especially on rock that's already featured like the stone in Valle Stretta. In my trad-climbing upbringing at the Gunks, this kind of ethical felony would get you sent to the gallows. To make matters even less appealing, the atmosphere was far from the lighthearted vibe you'd expect at a climbing event. One of the few jovial souls was our friend Jerry Moffatt, who couldn't compete due to elbow injuries but had come from England to watch. Between the weird vibe and the manufactured climbs, my appetite for the whole thing quickly shrank.

Wolfgang and I, along with other invitees, were not required to enter the qualifying round and got a free pass to the finals. We watched some climbers vying for a seat in the next day's final round, but then got bored and left the comp area. We found a nice boulder, facing away from the main scene, and booted up. There was no chalk on the fifteen-foot face, so we puzzled out the lower

Manolo Zanolla, Heinz Mariacher, Wolfgang Gullich (LtR) at the Sport Roccia competition in Bardonecchia, 1985

moves, pulling on small edges to reach a hard, committing move that was halting our progress. We were pleasingly immersed in the spirit of movement, taking turns trying to crack the problem, when Wolf noticed a small group gathering, not crowding us, but simply observing from a respectable distance. Wolfgang was famous and expected to do well in the competition, and when people caught wind that he was bouldering nearby, some wanted a preview. However, Wolfgang and I weren't interested in performing; the spell was broken. It would have been different if those who'd gathered were part of the process, trying the problem with us, but they weren't. They were just spectators. We took our shoes off and walked away.

That evening before the finals, the organizers held a press conference. Writers from the European climbing magazines were there, along with local journalists. Wolfgang, Jerry, and I were paraded out to give our thoughts about the competition. We were peppered with questions, translated from various languages into German or English. The interview was pretty confusing, but it quickly became apparent that Wolfgang and I were not giving the responses the sponsors or the press thought appropriate. We answered too many of their questions negatively: No, we didn't think this was very much fun. No, we didn't think this would prove who the best climber in the world is. No, we didn't think the competition brought out the best in climbers. It was the opposite, judging from the lack of smiles on the faces of so many competitors. We didn't see this event capturing the spirit of climbing in the least. This was an aberration.

Our "soul-climbing" attitude was completely outdated, as far as the interviewers were concerned. The questions got aggressive and heated: Why did we bother to come if we thought this was a bad move for climbing? Didn't we want to set a good example for the younger kids getting into the sport? We thought we had been, by calling the competition a circus. Wolfgang and I were amazed at the outbursts, but comic relief came from Jerry, who, with a couple of drinks in him, grabbed the mic and said, "Okay, folks, maybe it's time I sing you a little song!" The tent suddenly quieted down with the non-sequitur; nobody knew what to do aside from laugh as Jerry began singing. Wolfgang and I slipped out the door into the night.

Back at the car, we opened a bottle of wine and vented. I didn't think my mood could have gotten lower, but it had after the debacle at the press conference. Frank and Gabi had watched and said they thought we were going to be stoned to death in that tent. In a sense, we had been. We shared another bottle of wine. After that one emptied, Gabi and I retreated to our tent for the night. In the morning, my head was fuzzy from the drinking. I looked down toward the competition site. The human mass coming up the valley to watch the spectacle blew my mind. This was nothing

At Bardonecchia: Russ, Gabi, Wolfgang, and Jerry

like the small crowd from the day before, for the qualifiers. There were thousands of people here now. Television cameras were on the ground at the base of the comp routes, as well as on cherry pickers above, with more cameramen dangling on ropes. I felt nauseous.

The competition rules were simple. There was no isolation, as would become the norm in future competitions, where each competitor was forced to try the routes onsight, not gleaning beta from watching those who climbed prior. At Sportroccia, we were free to watch the performance of climbers preceding our turn. The format contained three difficulty routes and one speed route. Climbers had a preset amount of time to complete each difficulty route. If you fell, you could still go again after lowering to the ground, but there would be a deduction for the fall. The judges' scoring also had a "style" component, some subjective thing that no one could explain or quantify. It was up to the judges to decide who looked best on a route and award bonus points.

After he fell on the first route, Wolfgang untied and stormed off to his car, ignoring the announcer's call for his starting number for the next route. He was 100 percent over it. Since we were allowed to have our own belayers, I had my Gunks buddy, Frank, belay me. We climbed a lot together at home, and I was sure he wouldn't drop me. I also didn't want to use the tournament belay staff after seeing amount of slack they gave their climbers, making falls longer and more dramatic than necessary. Maybe that was a crowd pleaser, but I wasn't here to please anyone, especially not at the expense of my ankles.

As soon as I stepped up to the first route, I had a TV camera pointed at me from five feet away. I was nervous as hell to begin with and had a raging headache from the wine; I didn't need this, too. "Don't worry, Russ, I gotcha," Frank said, doing his best to calm me down. I grabbed the rock, over-gripping the holds out of sheer anxiety. My feet didn't want to stay put on the footholds either, adding to the pump in my arms. It seemed I had forgotten how to climb, and I fell about halfway up the first route. After a short rest I went back up, a little calmer this time. I climbed higher but ran out of time, and got lowered to the ground. The second route was harder, and I still hadn't recovered from the first route. I didn't complete that one either, but I no longer cared about the crowds, the cameras, or the overall craziness of the whole surreal scene. I didn't even give a shit about my performance. On the third route, I got an outright spanking. I fell at the first bolt. Jerry came over to give some helpful hints, but despite his insightful beta, I was fucked. I'd used what energy I had on the first two climbs and I never got past the second bolt on that last route. Thoroughly beat—both mentally and physically—I untied before my time was even up. I was over it. This sucked.

I still had the speed route. I mulled over bailing but decided to finish out this torture and not quit. My number was called, and I climbed the route—it was an easy jaunt, but I didn't rush. I just wanted to savor the climb, so I took my time. After I lowered and untied, a spectator grabbed my arm. "You could have climbed that MUCH faster!" he said.

"Yes, I could have," I replied, slipping away into the crowd.

After the competition ended, we stayed for the awards ceremony. We wanted to visit with some of our friends and congratulate those who did well. Stefan Glowacz, a very talented young German, won the men's division, and the French superstar Catherine Destivelle won the women's. Several men had tied by flashing all three routes and doing similarly well on the speed route, but the style equation won it for Stefan, and it was hard to argue the judges' decision. On the last of the difficulty routes, by far the hardest one, Glowacz pulled out the theatrics. He stopped right in the middle of the hardest moves, hanging from a fingertip edge, and removed a toothbrush from his chalk bag to brush residual chalk of the next couple of holds before continuing. The crowd roared in approval.

After the trophies and checks were awarded to the men's and women's top finishers, there were other prizes to give out. We had little idea what was being announced on the P.A. system because it was garbled, but there was no mistaking when my name was called. Wolf looked at me, surprised, and asked, "What could you have possibly won? Didn't you come in something like thirty-eighth place?" I had no idea either. My performance had sucked, and I was in the bottom third of the finishers. I went up on the stage and was handed a big trophy and a small day pack full of swag. I got some applause from the crowd, gave a weak wave of acknowledgement, and scampered off that stage as quickly as I could.

"Gabi, what does the plaque on the trophy say?" I asked. "It says you got this for coming the greatest distance to join the competition," she said. We all had a good laugh, the first one in a few days.

Before starting our drive back to West Germany, we joined Jerry and a small group of other friends for a pizza. We talked about the comp, our feelings, and the future of climbing, all in a big ball of rushed emotions. Our long drive through the night

Frank Minunni and Clune with "The Cup," Sport Roccia

remained just as animated. No one slept while we debated what
the Bardonecchia competition meant for the future of the sport.

I'd never seen Wolfgang like this. His raised voice was angry in
a visceral way I'd not heard before. Sure, I'd seen him get pissed
off in the past, and listened to him passionately debate climbing
ethics and style with other climbers around the kitchen table. But
this was something else. Wolfgang and I saw the competition in
different ways and argued about it into the night. We agreed that
it was not fun and that it didn't really prove who was "best"—and
what exactly did "best" mean anyway? But we disagreed on other
points, namely whether competition climbing had a future.

Wolfgang didn't think the competitions would last or be taken too seriously. I hoped he was right, given all the dour faces and environmental impact we'd witnessed, but I wasn't so sure. What about that huge crowd? The sponsors thought Sportroccia was a tremendous success, and most of the climbers seemingly embraced it, even if at the expense of fun. Stefan Glowacz put on a prize performance. And he won money—money! Something the climbing tribe had never seen before, just for going out and doing a little climbing. Plus, I argued, what sport in history hadn't eventually become overtly competitive? Climbing had always been competitive, just not in a formalized, objective way. I didn't see how climbing was going to go backward from the 1985 competition.

The largest problem I saw was the unabashed destruction of a pristine limestone cliff. Yes, Europe had cliffs all over, but would climbers tolerate the blasphemy of continual hold chipping to make new comp routes, especially if it came to their backyard areas? Would the tribe tolerate robbing the future of potentially difficult climbs no one could yet do, but that might eventually be possible? How selfish would today's climbers be in stealing the future of progression? (Fortunately for the rock, the advent of artificial walls was only a couple years away, making this point moot and allowing the competition scene to blow up in a way none of us foresaw then.)

However, as easy as it was for me to make these arguments, for Wolf, the stakes were much higher. I was a relative unknown at the comp, and there was no expectation for me to podium, or even do well. But Wolfgang was a star. Everyone knew that, just a few months earlier, he'd put up the world's first 5.14, in Australia. He was expected to do well—and probably win. The ramifications for him potentially went well beyond a bruised ego. He was a sponsored celebrity and he'd been knocked off his pedestal.

We were tired and cranky after the long ride, but everyone back home wanted the news. We talked incessantly about the competition with Kurt, Norbert, and the rest of the regular visitors to the house straight through the day and into the night. Already there was gossip of how Wolfgang had bailed on the comp and how other climbers had proven their worth by doing well, throwing into doubt Wolfgang's reign as king of the hill. What to do? Wolfgang and I wanted to get back to our normal climbing life, back to our routine: have our morning coffee, make a run to the bakery, and just go climbing.

My award, the large cup I got for traveling such a grand distance to attend Sportroccia, was worthy of sacrifice. During our short time in Bardonecchia, Wolfgang and I had sarcastically coined ourselves "Team Motivation." So Kurt, always the prankster, pried the little engraved plate off the base of my trophy and used a wood-burning tool to memorialize our team name instead. The "Team Motivation" cup would live on, but not in the house. It needed a new home. Wolf and I went out to Luisenwand, one of the scores of fine crags in the Frankenjura where Wolfgang had a new line in mind. He rappelled in to drill the protection bolts, and then added one more to the side, to which we promptly affixed the trophy.

Wolfgang was the first to redpoint the series of thin, technical moves on *Team Motivation*. When he got to the anchor and clipped the rope in, he inhaled deeply through his nose, gathered the snot off the back of his throat with a scraping exhale, and fired a huge loogie into the cup. A perfect three-pointer. I gave the spittoon a wide berth on my own redpoint. Despite the negative experience of the competition, the route was a reminder of what climbing meant to us. Not just hard routes, but the most important ingredient: the camaraderie of good friends at the crag. That day we tried hard, we had a few good laughs, and we climbed a new, difficult route. For us, that was the essence of the climbing experience.

I reluctantly departed the Frankenjura soon after we climbed *Team Motivation*. Bidding goodbye to the incomparable adventures with Wolfgang and Gabi's warm companionship sucked, but I was out of money. Wolfgang encouraged me to stay, saying, "Don't worry about the money—we will work something out and there are so many more routes to do!" He was right, of course, but it was about more than just being broke. I felt rootless and needed to get home to the Shawangunks to sort shit out.

The competition in Italy had thrown me for a loop. The discussions and arguments around the kitchen table at Wolfgang's house echoed in my head and led to more confusion and questions: *Was I committed to climbing? And what did that mean, exactly?* I'd spent well over five years on the road climbing, interspersed with short stints of work, living out of my folks' house. It was clear that sport climbing was where the pursuit of difficulty lay. *Did I have the balls to move to Europe, where the best of the best lived, where all the sport climbing was?* Competitions, I was sure, were going to be a big part of the climbing landscape from now on. *Did I want to start competing and try to make a living by climbing? Was I anywhere near good enough?*

I spent days doing a reality check, trying hard to be honest with myself. I was good, but not near as good as the very best

Making good use of the "Team Motivation" cup, Frankenjura

climbers. And I didn't like the competition or the environment surrounding it. If I didn't love that, there was no way I was going to do well. Another option, continuing down my current, meandering path, had its own landmines. I knew older climbers who had dropped out of the mainstream and became permanent dirtbags. Almost all of them had become cynical and bitter. Some became alcoholics. Many were essentially broke and homeless. I didn't want to end up there. I was twenty-six and had no intention of living in my childhood bedroom when I turned thirty, working sporadically while I bivvied at my folks' house. But get a job? Like, a real job? That thought was a nail straight into my heart, partially because I had no idea what I would do. I envisioned a cubical life, a mind-numbing 9-to-5 death trap of an existence. *Kill me now.* But I did know one thing that could delay the inevitable working-Joe life: go back to school and earn a graduate degree. I applied for a program in sport psychology at Teachers College, Columbia University and was accepted. Before fall semester, however, I still had some summer in front of me and more climbing to do.

I picked up work as a guide in the Gunks and house-sat in New Paltz for friends who left town for their own trips. Guiding provided enough cash to live on, and best of all, tons of free time for my own climbing agenda. The energy level was high. Besides my usual cohorts of talented climbing partners, we now had "the kids"—Scott Franklin, Jordy Mills, and Al Diamond—representing a new, youthful crew making their presence known with a slew of impressive ascents.

New routes were going up everywhere, many of them very hard, and often scary, but I knew that adhering to our traditional climbing style was holding us back from achieving European levels of technical difficulty. Europe was miles ahead of the United States now. Still, as much as I enjoyed sport climbing and the freedom it gave to try really hard without endangering myself, I saw a beauty in and relevance to the idea of a mental challenge—keeping your wits above questionable protection, knowing there was a real consequence for a fall. There was even something romantic about the teamwork the traditional yo-yo style demanded. When we started from the ground, heading up into the unknown, the experience created a bond between everyone working to move the rope up the cliff. Sport climbing had no unknowns since the bolts were placed on rappel, the holds quickly became pre-marked with chalk, and there was little teamwork. The redpoint style was mostly a solitary mission and not a shared communion of the rope. But the yo-yo style had the same odds of survival as an iceberg in Florida. It was a vestige of the past. Competitions aside, the quest, the evolution of rock climbing was becoming about difficulty, not danger. I started shedding some of the old ways myself, even on my home turf.

While I continued with some of the traditional ways, at least as far as using clean climbing protection, one tactic I gladly embraced was hangdogging. Being called a "hangdog," a cliffside pejorative in the States, was meaningless to me. Hanging on the rope to feel the holds and practice moves after falling was simply efficient. I also liked the redpoint idea, the purity of a bottom-to-top lead ascent, placing all the protection as you went. I used this concept with a few first ascents that summer, but not always. Depending on whom I was climbing with, we engaged in different formats. Some of my older partners were fine with the old yo-yo style; some wanted a more modern redpoint style. Some of us even experimented with placing bolts on rappel in the Gunks, bringing true sport climbing front and center. The result was a short-lived war between traditionalists, who quickly chopped the bolts, and sport-climbing advocates, who just as quickly replaced them. In

1986, the Mohonk Preserve, owners of most of the Shawangunk climbing areas, declared any further bolting illegal, along with the use of pitons. It was a preserve, after all, not a war zone for petulant climbers to scar up the rock with repeated holes drilled for bolts and chip marks where chisels had been used to remove them. If the climbing community couldn't figure it out amongst themselves, then the Mohonk Preserve would do it for them. That settled it. The Gunks would remain a traditional climbing area, and to a degree, the bolting ban sealed it in amber. Hard routes would get done now and then, either as top ropes or as heady trad lines, but never again would the Gunks define leading-edge climbing in the world in terms of pure difficulty.

HOMAGE AND COMING TO TERMS WITH A NEW WORLD ORDER

"Life is being on the wire; everything else is just waiting."

—Karl Wallenda

On the morning of August 28, 1985, I puttered up the hill on US 44/NY 55 in my pickup and parked along the road below the Uberfall. There were no other cars, no climbers hanging around yet. It was much too early, but that didn't matter to me. That day, I wasn't there to meet anyone. I had a plan. I pulled my mountain bike out of the pickup's bed along with a small day pack of gear and went up the stone steps to the old carriage-road system that wound around the cliffs.

The late-summer morning felt pleasant, with a coolness raising goosebumps on my skin and whispering of fall's imminent arrival. I inserted a cassette tape by The Smiths in my Sony Walkman, hit play, and started the three-mile ride to Sky Top, my favorite cliff in the Gunks. The ride started flat and easy, the shale surface crunching beneath my tires as I rode below the Trapps, passing favorite sections of cliff filled with routes I'd done many times. There was the *McCarthy Wall*, with its palette of orange, brown, and gray streaks, and the large Andrew Boulder that overhangs the carriage road. Over the years, I'd camped underneath its protective cover on many a rainy night.

High above, the cliff glistened white in the brightening sun. The road turned away from the Trapps as the cliff tapered in height. Passing over a small bridge, I turned left into a steep uphill grind, pushing hard into the pedals as Johnny Marr's melancholy guitar riffs echoed in my ears, melding with Morrisey's singular voice. Staccato percussion helped me forget how long the hill was and keep my cadence on the pedals.

At the crest, the angle eased and I glided toward my destination. The deciduous forest of oak, maple, and birch dropped away on the hillside to the east, rolling into the green fields of the Wallkill Valley. Above me was the Sky Top cliff. I got glimpses of the rock between trees as I passed more climbs I'd done repeatedly. *The Crack of Bizarre Delights* was one of those, a prominent, jutting visor at the top of the cliff, resembling the bill of a baseball cap.

Since my return from West Germany, I'd had time to reflect on my future, and that future, I'd finally concluded, would not involve partaking in what I'd seen In Bardonecchia; I was not going to pack up my belongings and move to Europe. With competition climbing, something wild was being tamed, something pure now tainted by forces more interested in the business of climbing rather than its raw spirit. It was not for me, and knowing that I didn't like it also meant I would never work hard enough to be relevant in the game and make a living as a climber. I'd be going back to school in a couple weeks, and my climbing time was about to be limited to weekends and holidays, not involve grand voyages to distant countries for months on end. Still, I wouldn't have traded the previous magical climbing years for anything, and before classes started, I had plans for one more big climb: a free solo of *Supercrack.*

Even with the acceptance of sport-climbing tactics in Europe and with the old, traditional methods of rock climbing on life support, one style of climbing was then and still is now widely considered the essence of mastery: the free solo. And for good reason—soloing requires not only the physical ability to do the route, but most importantly, the mental control to overcome paralyzing fear. The consequences of failure can be fatal.

In the Gunks, a friendly game of "one-upmanship soloing" erupted on the scene that summer. Jeff Gruenberg and I bantered about what the raddest solos in the Gunks would be. Many good climbers soloed routes regularly, usually climbing well within their limits and rarely exceeding 5.10 or so. I had a small circuit I did, which sprinkled in a couple 5.11s and one 5.12, all with their cruxes close to the ground and more like highball boulder problems, with the worst outcome of a fall likely just a broken limb. But the climbs Jeff and I thought about were different.

Of course, they had to be classics. We settled on a few that absolutely made that list: *Foops,* a nine-foot roof at solid 5.11, its crux fifty feet above a talus field; *Open Cockpit,* a forty-foot technical face climb rated 5.11+; and *Supercrack,* a hard 5.12, the epitome of mastery of the game, at least as far as we were concerned. While roped, we would do these three climbs with a regularity that made them rote exercises, to the point where I could climb up, back down, and then back up *Supercrack* without a break. Jeff broke the ice with a solo of *Foops.* The talk was becoming action. I went next with a solo of *Open Cockpit.* Two down, one to go.

Way back in 1974, Steve Wunsch spent so many days working on *Supercrack,* that one of his partners quipped it should be named "Wunsch Upon a Climb." When Wunsch finally climbed *Supercrack,* he established one of the world's most difficult free climbs for the era. The achievement is respected to this day, especially when considering that Wunsch didn't have the advantages conferred by easy-to-place spring-loaded camming devices or modern, precise, sticky-soled rock shoes.

The line of *Supercrack* is perfect: the fissure splits the middle of a sixty-foot pinnacle of orange quartz conglomerate, climbing through alluring black and white water streaks. At first glance, *Supercrack* looks relatively easy, its overhanging, strenuous nature not apparent until you pull onto the wall. Then, after it has sucked you in, it chucks all kinds of problems at you in quick succession. I knew exactly what lay ahead of me: The very start of the crack is wide enough to stuff your hands into, providing a couple of good hand jams and security. Then the crack narrows down to an awkward size, "rattly fingers," which is too big for solid fingerlocks but too small for hand jams. Adding to the difficulty is a paucity of good foot holds, meaning you must press your toe tips into the thin crack or splay them on the sides on tiny edges. Good technique and balance are the ticket to getting through this part of the climb, the technical crux.

Now comes a small overhang. Here, contortionist moves and difficult hand shuffling up the crack lead to a large, flat handhold; this jug is the best hold since leaving the ground, but with your feet still under the overhang on poor holds, you can't stop for long. You have to keep moving, feet pressing against one side of the crack while your hands work in opposition on the other side, laybacking powerfully over the obstacle to stand up on the jug, where you win a good rest before the last twenty feet. The crack thins down now, less than an inch wide and only accepting fingertips in a series of strenuous moves that lead to a large, positive-feeling handhold and the final, easier ten feet to the top of the pinnacle. Most climbers find *Supercrack* feels a lot longer than its mere sixty feet.

At the base of the route, I took a seat on a large slab. Looking up at the crack, I envisioned each move, each hold, every nuance of body position I would need to climb fluidly. Still, I wanted to warm up and see how it felt before I committed to a solo. I fixed my rope and rappelled the line, feeling the jams on the upper section. They were crisp and rough, the crack still cool from the previous night's air, just how I wanted. Back at the base, I rigged up a self-belay system, put on my climbing shoes, making sure each toe found its correct place in the tight confines, and set off. I only took a couple minutes to dash up *Supercrack*. It felt solid. The holds felt big, the finger jams secure; it felt *easy*.

I stepped up to the start of *Supercrack* once again, now with no rope. A fall from the crux section before the overhang would be bad—dropping onto the jumbled, sloped talus below would mean at least broken limbs. A fall higher up would be certain death. But I wasn't going to fall, and I knew that. I brushed my hand along the soles of my shoes, clearing away any dirt and grime. After dipping my fingers into my chalk bag and rubbing the powder into my hands, I slotted my left hand into the first jam, took a couple deep breaths, and started climbing.

A couple minutes later, at the top of the pinnacle, I sat and gazed out over Wallkill Valley, across the flats to the outline of the buildings in New Paltz. My sprint up the climb had left me hyper-adrenalized and slightly shaky, but I felt zero fatigue. I knew that *Supercrack* marked the hardest climb I would ever do without a rope and, in that sense, a retirement of sorts, at least from full-time climbing. Graduate school started in two weeks.

CLOSE ENCOUNTERS; A QUEST FOR SPEED AND A CULTURAL TRAIN WRECK

"The rules are simple: they lie to us, we know they're lying, they know we know they're lying, but they keep lying to us, and we keep pretending to believe them."

—*Elena Gorokhova,*

I first met Todd Skinner and Beth Wald in December of 1984 at the desert climbing area of Hueco Tanks, outside El Paso, Texas, a climber's playground of superb boulders and walls featuring pockets of all sizes to grab onto and pull through steep features. Todd was a gregarious and determined man, with a plan to be one of the best climbers and the work ethic to make it happen. He also shared my passion for discovery of new places to rock climb. We hit it off well and agreed it would be a great experience to go to Russia, mostly because we knew almost nothing about what we might find. The place was huge—there had to be good rock somewhere.

At the time, Russia was part of the USSR, under Communist control and not easily visited by tourists, at least not tourists like us, who'd want the freedom to roam and do it on a dirtbag budget. Beth spoke and wrote some Russian, and got to work researching a possible climbing trip. She found the only way we could climb in Russia without getting arrested, assuming we were able to get in the country at all, was to partake in an official, government-sanctioned event. The only option was a speed-climbing competition the USSR held every two years, a longstanding tradition that mostly involved Eastern Bloc countries. The United States had never been a participant, and that posed a problem. We couldn't just assign ourselves as the US team. The Soviets said we needed to have the blessing of the American Alpine Club (AAC) and to be recognized by them as the officially sanctioned team.

While the idea of going to Russia for a competition was not what we were looking for, we decided the trip would be worth it, and we might even get some real climbing done. The first step was getting the AAC to back us. Luckily, the president at the time, Jim McCarthy, was a friend and was happy to back our plan. The issue was, he needed board approval. He couldn't just unilaterally call us the official US Speed Climbing Team. In this era of the Cold War, there was resistance, especially among some of the older and more conservative board members, who worried that we could potentially embarrass the United States in front of the Soviets by underperforming. Given my underwhelming competition résumé and the fact that we didn't know shit about speed climbing, their concerns rung true enough. Still, Jim succeeded in getting us a letter to send to the Soviets. As far as Russia was concerned, me, Todd, Beth, and the talented Colorado climber Dan Michael were now the 1986 American Alpine Club–approved USA Speed Climbing Team.

Before the competition, Todd, Beth, and Dan went to Europe to climb, but I couldn't join them since I had one final semester to complete my master's degree. We planned to rendezvous in Moscow, but my flights got delayed and I arrived in Moscow a day late. I caught a jet to Yalta the next morning. As I deplaned, I noticed a beautiful young woman in a white jacket waiting on the tarmac for the arriving passengers. *Wouldn't it be great if she was here to pick me up?* I thought. Turned out, Nina was—she was Team USA's translator. Nina escorted me to a waiting car, and we drove to meet my teammates.

"God damn your eyes! It's good to see ya!" Todd said as he grabbed my hand with his usual enthusiastic greeting, pumping my arm up and down as if he was waiting for water to pour from my mouth. He and the others were in the common room of the dorm-style complex for the competitors, just a short drive from the seaside cliffs where the event was being held.

Todd filled me in on details of the competition he'd learned so far, during the practice round the previous day. While we were

Team USA at the USSR Speed Climbing Event, Yalta, 1986
Left to right: Nina (interpreter) Todd Skinner, Beth Wald, Dan Michael, Clune

Built for speed, Soviet style

required to have four members, each team would have only two males and one female climb, while the fourth climber served as the coach. In our case, Dan had injured his wrist earlier in the trip, so he would be our "coach." There were nine other countries there, all from Eastern Europe save us, the West Germans, and the Japanese. I knew the Germans, one being my good friend Norbert Sandner, a housemate of Wolfgang's, and Stefan Glowacz, the young stud who'd won at Bardonecchia the previous year. I also knew one of the Japanese guys from my trip there the year before. Otherwise, the remainder of the climbers were mysteries to us. Few of them had ever traveled outside their own countries, much less anywhere west of the Iron Curtain, and we knew nothing about the climbing in their home countries—nations like Poland, Romania, and Bulgaria.

The competition took place on a few limestone cliffs of varying height. The events included a "short" toprope route with about a hundred feet of climbing and a "long" toprope that was twice as tall. Beth's routes were different than the ones Todd and I were required to climb, and supposedly a little easier. Bright-red stripes of paint curving up the cliff defined the routes; straying beyond the lines or falling meant instant disqualification for that climb.

Each morning, the officials held a meeting, letting us know the agenda for the day. The room buzzed with translators relaying information to the various teams. Nina—whom I found so alluring, with her high cheekbones and shoulder-length brown hair—worked hard for us, posing our questions to the judges as we sought clarity on the rules—of which there were a lot, beyond simply not crossing the painted lines. There were rules concerning climbing "safely," many of which appeared oxymoronic. Take the belaying, for starters. For the topropes, the official belayers were two very large men who I doubted ever had previous cause to touch a rope, other than while doing farm chores. They sucked in the slack hand over hand as if playing tug-of-war, with absolutely no belay device, pulling the rope as fast as the climber could move. Thick leather gloves protected them from rope burns when they lowered the climber at a heartbeat-skipping clip, slowing the descent just before the ground. It was horrifyingly scary the first time and just slightly less so on ensuing lowers.

On the first day of competition, we gathered at a crag on the Black Sea. A chilly breeze flowed off the water, and clouds darkened the sky, threatening to drench us. The cliff was a nice hunk of steep rock, featuring an appealing corner system at mid-height. In much of Europe, this cliff would be riddled with bolted sport climbs, but here in the USSR, it had no bolts but instead two parallel red lines showing the boundaries of the climb, with a large red flag at the top signaling the end.

The disparity between the teams from the West and those from the East was a lesson in our vastly different economic systems. The gear the Soviet climbers used looked like stuff dredged up from a construction site, or perhaps bequeathed to them by nineteenth-century mountaineers. Many climbed in simple chest harnesses, not something I'd think very comfortable or safe in the event of a fall. Some had helmets that looked like they came from a military surplus outlet or were possibly carved from giant coconut shells. The "climbing shoes" they sported were *golashkis*, essentially rubber rain boots that resembled Totes. A small crowd of spectators, along with a throng of reporters and TV cameras, had gathered to view the antics. The Russians were especially interested in us Americans. I was called up for an interview with an announcer, who translated where I came from, what I did for a living, and the like. I got a nice round of applause as he thanked me and then called up Todd.

Interviewer: "So, Todd, where in America do you live? "

"I live in WHY-O-MING," Todd replied, slowly emphasizing every syllable of his home state.

Interviewer: "Ah, Wyoming. But where is Wyoming?"

Todd: "It is in the West."

Interviewer: "Ah, the West! And what do you do in Wyoming, in the West?"

Todd: "I am a COWBOY!"

The crowd went nuts with applause and hoots when the translation was piped over the loudspeakers. It was perfect, and Team USA became a fan favorite—after the home-team Russians, of course.

In the evenings, we were left to amuse ourselves, and we did, often in tandem with the Germans and Japanese. We frequented a dance hall and bar in a nearby fancy hotel. Nina did her best to keep us out of trouble, but one evening we were unceremoniously bounced off the dance floor and kicked out of the building after the authorities decided slam dancing was not a good mix with the hotel's paying guests.

Todd and I completed our two topropes and managed to not get disqualified, though we weren't especially speedy. Beth fared well on her first route, but on her second she got disqualified for a fall. Todd and I had one more event, a four-pitch route on which we'd swing leads. We could use any aid we wanted—pulling on the fixed gear was allowed. Our score was based on both ascent time and rappel time back to the ground. We were free to watch the other teams preceding us do the route, and we learned some

Todd Skinner & Russ doing whatever needed to move fast. Photo: Beth Wald

tricks. The second pitch required a pendulum around an arête to gain the belay, so we noted how far to lower the leader to make the swing work on the first attempt. We also noticed that the Russians had exactly the right amount of rope. The pitches were all the same length, about twenty meters, and there was never any slack for them to wrangle at belays, losing precious time. Meanwhile, other teams were adding seconds to every pitch, dealing with their fifty-meter, standard-length ropes. We asked if we could borrow the Russians' rope, and they agreed to let us.

Todd took off on the first pitch and got to the belay in no time, yarding on gear and moving fast. I did the same while following, remaining at the belay only a moment to grab gear from Todd for the next pitch. Todd lowered me to the right spot for the pendulum so quickly I thought maybe he'd dropped me. I swung around the arête, grabbed the next belay anchor on my first go, and gave Todd a yell; he immediately let loose from his belay to join me. The remaining pitches went just as smoothly as we hauled ass to the top. Now it was time to rappel. We'd watched some of the other teams zip down at speeds that made me look away, sure they would splatter. Todd and I were more cautious. I thought we'd done well on the way up, and on the way down had, I believed, descended speedily but certainly not recklessly. As it turned out, we had the second fastest ascent time, after the Russians, but the slowest descent time of any team.

After the dust settled and the results came in, somehow Team USA surprisingly came in third place, behind the Russians and the Poles. Our last evening in Yalta was an awards celebration, sharing dinner and laughs with the other competitors. After a few beers, I was ready for bed. I excused myself and went up to my room. Nina joined me, saying she was tired too. Her room was across the hall from mine. When I said good night, turning to go to my door, she took me by the arm and swiftly pulled me into her room. She shut the door behind us, wrapped her arms around me, and gave me a lingering kiss. As soon as it ended, she opened the door, checked that nobody else was in the hallway, and gently pushed me out of her room, closing her door quietly. I stood in the hall for a moment, wondering what just happened, knowing she'd just taken a risk.

On the flight back to Moscow the following day, Nina sat next to me. She would look around once in awhile to see that no one was watching, and then take my hand in hers and squeeze before quickly releasing it. I was most definitely infatuated. Nina left us at the airport, giving us formal farewell handshakes, me included. However, I had something my friends did not: her phone number and address. I knew I was going to return.

I jumped through substantial bureaucratic hoops to visit Nina right after Christmas in 1986, including paying an exorbitant rate to stay in a "deluxe" tourist hotel in downtown Moscow, which essentially allowed the authorities to keep tabs on me. The National Hotel had probably been nice back in the Tsarist era, but it hadn't seen much updating since. My drab room was poorly lit and painted pink, with darker blotches where water damage had stained the walls. The tiles on the bathroom floor were mostly loose, and the mattress was as supportive as over-boiled pasta. I'd stayed in fancier Motel 6s. I walked into the bone-numbing air outside the hotel to a pay phone to call Nina, and we met outside the Bolshoi Theatre, not far from my place. She greeted me with an embrace, a kiss, and a cold nose. Her face was barely visible through the fur-lined hat she'd pulled down to her eyebrows and the scarf covering her chin, but I could see she was happy to see me.

The next two weeks were a blur of boring days, since Nina had to work, and long nights spent together. As far as I knew, the purpose of my visit was a secret to the authorities. I spent my days exploring the frozen streets of Moscow and using the excellent and cheap subway system. Each stop had a different theme and look, complete with sculptures and other artwork. With little else to do, I made a point of visiting every single one of them. The stations were stunningly immaculate, and there were always a couple of women mopping mud and melting snow off the floors. I understood that Nina had to be careful. Her work as a translator represented a very good job in the Soviet system, and she told me she could get into serious trouble if she was found hanging out with an American. So, our evening meetings happened in safe places like her friends' homes. We usually went out for dinners, but always in a group where I was less noticeable. The conversation around the tables in public places was in Russian and lost to me. But in the safety of someone's living room, Nina and her friends freely spoke English.

There was excitement in the social circles Nina introduced me to, mostly artists, writers, and what would be considered the intelligentsia. Gorbachev was in office and had rolled out his policies of *glasnost* (openness) and *perestroika* (restructuring). The old Soviet system was broken, and change was in the air. People were gingerly testing the waters with their speech and art, finding they could do things unimaginable just a couple years beforehand. Still, Nina acted with caution. While the temperature outside continued to plunge, my affection for her only heated up. We laughed a lot, mixing our conversations between the serious and the frivolous: *What did she think of Gorbachev? What were her favorite foods? What did she think America was like?* Conversations came easily. When I left Moscow, the temperature was forty below zero, but I knew that I'd be back to see Nina again.

A few weeks before that trip to Moscow to see Nina, the American Alpine Club had held its annual gathering in Denver. I attended to give a slideshow on my recent travels and ran into Maria Cranor almost as soon as I got to the event. Maria was the marketing director for Chouinard Equipment, the US's premier climbing gear manufacturer at the time, and Yvon Chouinard's original company before he started his outdoor-clothing venture, Patagonia.

Maria and I had met on several occasions, haphazardly crossing paths during our climbing trips, and we got along well. She possessed a powerful personality, backed by a sharp intellect few could match. We'd had great conversations on a host of topics, ranging from psychology to physics to climbing ethics. After a hello hug, Maria dropped the glowing smile and gave me a serious look. She knew I'd just finished grad school and asked me what I was doing now. I explained I was in a limbo of sorts, not yet sure of what came next. She asked if I knew Peter Metcalf, who held the general-manager role at Chouinard Equipment. Though Yvon still owned the company, his attention was very much focused on Patagonia, and he'd hired Metcalf a few years earlier to run the hardware side of the business. I knew of Peter—he'd made some serious first ascents on Alaskan peaks that I'd read about—but had never met him. Maria then said, "We want to hire you." When I asked doing what, she said Peter would tell me. He was also at the AAC meeting.

Peter and I met just a little while afterward in the hallways of the event venue, between presentations. He said that Maria had spoken highly of me and thought I'd be a good fit at Chouinard. Peter explained that they needed someone to run and build Chouinard's export sales program. *This is going nowhere,* I thought. I told Peter I didn't know a thing about exports or sales, but he remained unmoved. He said I must know a lot of people, being as well traveled as I was, and asked if I could learn the business. I replied I probably could, but did he really want someone to learn on the go? Peter said he was more interested in hiring people who would be a good cultural fit as opposed to possessing a particular skill set, and so, not long after returning from Moscow, I flew out to the Chouinard headquarters in Ventura, California.

The tour of the Chouinard Equipment offices took about five minutes. A short staircase led up to a narrow porch with a sign by the door that read "Friends of the Ventura River." There was no indication that these were the offices of Chouinard Equipment, the storied manufacturer of top-shelf American climbing gear. Inside, the space was mostly one great, big room, with Metcalf and Maria's work area in an office in the back. A receptionist sat at her station, facing the entryway. She took incoming calls, forwarding them to one of the three women working customer service at old desks and folding tables with computer terminals and phones. I was introduced to everyone before Peter escorted me across the parking lot to the "big house", the home of Patagonia's staff, to have lunch at the company cafeteria. As we ate, Peter talked about what my role would be if I took the job. He seemed confident that I was going to come work for him, but I wasn't so sure.

I again voiced my hesitation, but Metcalf reiterated what he'd told me in Denver—that the company's main focus was to find personalities that were good fits to the company culture. I asked about compensation. Peter gave me a lowball offer, one that almost had me busting out with a laugh, until I saw he was serious. I'd made more money part-time day-trading while in grad school. After some light negotiation, we reached a deal. *What the hell?* I thought. *Might as well give it a shot.* I agreed to come out to California, and promised him I'd stick it out for at least a full year.

Back home in New York, I spent a couple weeks saying goodbye to friends and packing my scant belongings—my climbing gear, stereo, records, and books—into my van. On a cold January morning, I shut the door to my bedroom at my folks' house with a pit in my stomach. I knew I would never live at home again and that I was at the end of an era. I started up my van and headed west, for the first time in years traveling into an unknown future that wasn't a climbing adventure.

My "desk" at the Chouinard office was a plastic table tucked against a windowless white wall, and had a phone and a computer terminal on top of it. I had no idea what to do, and neither did I get much instruction from the other three reps, each of whom happily dumped their meager and—I soon found—mostly ignored export responsibilities on my desk. Luckily, one of the office staff had a good handle on the basics and pointed me in the right direction, telling me which accounts to prioritize and which were pains in the ass. I wasn't long before I became well versed in letters of credit, freight forwarders, foreign exchange rates, and export-pricing guidelines. To my surprise, the work was interesting and thought provoking.

Chouinard Equipment was a sink-or-swim environment. I had

plenty of leash to make decisions and end up with either the credit or blame. No one was looking over my shoulder—most of the time, in fact, no one was looking at all. On my first overseas trip, only three weeks into my job, Metcalf bailed on accompanying me to the huge ISPO trade show in Munich. I was on my own, aside from being allowed to use the Patagonia booth there for meetings. But there was an upside to not having my boss there. Wolfgang was around, along with Norbert and other European climber friends. At the end of each day, we'd walk from the show to a nearby Italian restaurant and crowd into a big booth in the back, catching up over pizza and wine for hours.

In spring 1987, I returned to Moscow to visit Nina. I'm not sure she'd believed me when I told her I would come back. It remained a hassle to visit the Soviet Union, despite a few relaxed regulations. I called Nina often between my visits, but this process was snarled in red tape as well. I had to get an operator to connect me to her number, then wait a day or two for a call back from another operator, who gave me a time frame to be by my phone to receive Nina's call. What's worse, Soviet authorities were almost surely listening in, so our conversations were stilted and unsatisfying.

Still, I was excited about seeing her again and wondered about next steps. It was impossible to continue this long-distance relationship, so if our romance was going to work, I'd need to bring her to the United States and get married. I wasn't sure I was ready to do that, and I hoped for more clarity during this trip. At the National Hotel, I got escorted to the exact same room I'd occupied in the winter, but it was marginally less depressing now with spring daylight filtering through the windows.

The May afternoon was cool and pleasant as Nina and I

walked at a leisurely pace down the Moscow sidewalks. She was impressed that I had come back, even a little surprised. She was more relaxed than during my previous visit, just months earlier, possibly due to the change in the political winds in Russia. Shortly into our stroll, she told me my return could only mean one thing: that I wanted to get married.

Whoa. I was not at all prepared for that, at least not put so bluntly and only a few minutes into our reunion. In a panic that I hoped wasn't apparent to her, I steered the conversation to safer topics like what Nina had been doing over the last few months, delaying the marriage discussion for now.

We visited Nina's friends, and they filled me in on how much had happened in Moscow since my January visit. The system was truly changing, and they were giddy with a freedom of expression they'd never enjoyed before. I was quite content to be in these group settings where Nina and I had no time to talk about marriage, and with each passing day I became more and more doubtful about bringing her to the United States. Other than a mutual attraction, we had nothing in common, and I'm not sure why I hadn't seen this sooner, other than I was smitten with her. She was an urban creature, with urban sensibilities, and would never embrace my rough-around-the-edges climbing lifestyle. I couldn't picture her at a crag, climbing with me or having any fun in my natural environment.

One week into my visit, she told me that once we were married, I would become a family man, and so would need to prepare for new responsibilities in my life. *"Family man?" What was that supposed to mean?* I pictured things I had worked to escape since childhood: a boring suburban life, kids, a mind-numbing job, chasing money, amassing possessions. One evening shortly thereafter we got into a fight, and Nina stormed off in a huff, leaving me to return to the hotel earlier than I expected to. I waited to hear from Nina again, but my hotel phone never rang, and I tried only once to call her and didn't get an answer, which was, admittedly, a relief. I didn't want to go any further. I neither saw nor heard from Nina again for the remainder of my time in Russia, instead spending time with acquaintances and learning more about the changes in Moscow.

I flew back to California in time to catch Todd Skinner and his traveling companions passing through the area. Todd was giving slideshows about our trip to the Soviet speed-climbing event at local venues, and we had ample time to chat and catch up. Just a few days after my return, I received a letter from Nina, her missive arriving amazingly quickly from Russia. In all the previous months she never sent so much as a postcard, telling me on the phone that it was too difficult and possibly dangerous. I had believed her, but apparently, those worries evaporated when it came to posting hate mail. I read Todd the four-page letter, in which she excoriated me for leaving her behind and hoped I died a miserable, painful death.

"Well," Todd surmised with his best cowboy comeback, "guess ya dodged a bullet there, pardner."

CHANGES; IT'S ALWAYS LATER THAN YOU THINK

"You only live once, but if you do it right, once is enough."

—Mae West

After my first year at Chouinard, my job morphed, with added responsibilities. Metcalf still had me running the export program, which was growing nicely, and he decided that since I was from New York, I should represent the brand to our accounts back East as well. Between trade shows in Europe, distributor visits in Asia and Australia, and driving up and down the East Coast, I was hardly home, so I moved out of my townhouse and into a buddy's garage. My friends had a laugh about that, but the garage-turned-bedroom was all I needed in the pleasant climate of Southern California. On the sporadic occasions I was home, I woke early to surf, grabbed breakfast on my way to the office, and in the evenings went out to dinner with friends, so I almost never used my kitchen. I once went an eighteen-month stretch without cooking a single meal there. As tiring as my vagabond lifestyle was, the big plus was climbing in a ton of really great places—I'd always bake in "sanity breaks" for climbing, no matter where I was.

In the heart of the Appalachians, I was especially taken by the explosion of new routes at the New River Gorge in West Virginia, where excellent sport climbs were going up on the bullet-hard Nuttall sandstone as fast as the bolts could be slammed in. On my trips back that way I squeezed in extra-long stints at the New, loving how it offered both technical climbs on vertical and gently overhanging walls and wildly overhanging cave routes.

The Southern boys Doug Reed and Porter Jarrard were among the many developers active at the New in the late 1980s and early 1990s. I found Doug's routes especially to my liking, and his laidback personality as well. Not only did Doug have an eye for great lines, he also bolted them well—enough to keep you safe, but never so many clips that you felt like you were in a climbing gym. Doug was just a tad taller than me at six-foot-three and had a more muscular physique, earning him the nickname "Appollo Reed." His torso also sprouted long arms that put my considerable reach to shame. Doug was from Jackson, Mississippi, and when we first met, he lived out of an ancient Volvo during the spring and fall climbing seasons, returning to Jackson to work when the summer humidity was at its worst and winter's cold, short gray days were at their grimmest. He eventually upgraded to renting a clapboard shack of dubious construction within the four blocks that defined "downtown" Fayetteville, the nearest town, seated atop the rim of the gorge. I could rely on a phone call from Doug, usually in March and September, inviting me to stay with him. I enjoyed the hospitality and his company, and there was some utility from his perspective as well: when I joined him and his girlfriend, Angie, at the shack, we had a higher ratio of humans to rats in the dwelling.

Doug had a wonderfully mellifluous, baritone drawl that was only enhanced by his learned diction. Doug had spent his younger years in elite private schools, and it showed. He could find the most elegant way to phrase a mundane expression. Where my

Russ on "The Pod," New River Gorge, West Virgina
Photo: Eddie Whittemore

quip around the breakfast table might be, "Hey, weather's looking good; we should get going," Doug would say something like, "Russ, I believe the weather gods are favoring us today. I'd suggest we quickly seize this opportunity for a fine outing of rock climbing. Would you not agree?"

Doug also had a dry, subtle wit he wasn't shy about employing, to great comic effect. We once had an acquaintance, another denizen of the New River scene, give us a blow-by-blow run-down of his recent training regimen. After each description of some eye-popping performance of strength, Doug responded with a drawn out, "Really?!" After our friend finished his boast, there was a moment of silence before Doug opined, "Well, that's truly incredible. With all that strength, you surely must be the most underachieving climber the sport has ever known!"

On a beautiful October afternoon, I was in the gorge at Endless Wall, on the north rim, with Doug and Porter. Doug had bolted a stunning, orange and black tiger-striped wall that he'd dubbed *Quinsana Plus*, so named for an anti-fungal foot powder Doug was using inside his climbing shoes. He and Porter were vying for the first redpoint of the route, which climbed a series of small edges via unrelenting, bouldery sequences up the gently overhanging face. The cliff was buzzing with a dozen or so climbers doing their own routes and watching the Doug and Porter show. Earlier in the year, Porter had adopted a stray mutt he'd found near his home in Greensboro, North Carolina. Poochie was not an attractive animal. He was small, around twenty pounds, with short, stout legs and a barrel-shaped body. Guessing his parental heritage was a fool's errand. Most of us agreed that Poochie was a mistake of genetics that only Porter found attractive. His fur had the texture of a wire brush; you'd only touch it if you were trying to scrape something off your hands. Plus, he smelled terrible. But what

Poochie lacked in attractiveness he made up for with his limitless libido. No leg was off limits to his lustful thrusting.

Two friends from Atlanta, Dave and Emy, came to join us at the crag that afternoon. They also had a dog, a female named Roxy. She was a pure-bred boxer, and Emy treated her like a princess. Dave and Emy were descending the ladders from the rim to the base of the cliff, Dave leading the way and holding Roxy in the crook of one arm while negotiating the ladder. When Dave got to the bottom, unaware of Poochie's presence, he let Roxy loose. Well, it turned out Roxy was in heat. Poochie snapped to attention and bolted over to Roxy, his canine manhood instantly unsheathed. Roxy yelped when Poochie charged. Emy, now on the last rungs of the ladder, saw what was about to happen and screamed. Dave whipped around to see Roxy growling and yapping at Poochie as he ran her in circles, her tail tucked tighter than a chastity belt. Dave was yelling at Roxy, Porter was yelling at Poochie, and Emy was screaming in horror while the rest of us looked on, laughing our heads off.

Dave finally got ahold of Roxy, just as Poochie seemed poised to consummate their union. Porter grabbed Poochie as well, firmly holding the dog's back to his chest as Poochie squirmed and growled. Years of sexual frustration came to a head, and Poochie ejaculated like a fire hose from Porter's arms, sending an arcing stream of semen cascading through the air. The pulsing rain shower of doggie DNA landed squarely on the back of Dave's jacket while he tended to his traumatized boxer. Dave was unaware of the defiling at first, making us laugh ever harder. Eventually I was able to catch my breath and let Dave know he'd want to burn that jacket.

On Monday, April 17, 1989, I was in the Red River Gorge, Kentucky. The Red was a total backwater then, nothing remotely close to the bustling international sport-climbing destination it is today. There were very few amenities at the time, aside from the Natural Bridge State Resort Park dining room and a depressing collection of roadside attractions, including a reptile zoo and tacky souvenir shops. Bolted sport routes were still a few years into the future here, so the Red remained an infrequently visited, diehard traditional climbing area with a tiny core of climbing locals from the nearby Lexington area. Visiting climbers were as rare as a cold Kentucky summer day.

I hadn't come here to climb, and only made the four-hour drive from the New, where I'd been enjoying myself immensely, out of professional obligation. Even though I had purchased a 1984 edition of a guidebook to the Red a couple years before, none of the routes looked especially interesting and I'd been warned that the Corbin sandstone was friable and subpar. Nothing I'd heard from the few people I knew who'd been there made it sound worth a trip. But a small climbing store on Kentucky Route 11, near the entrance to the State Park, had contacted me with a request to sell Chouinard Equipment gear. Local climber Martin Hackworth and a couple of his friends had opened their shop called Search for Adventure. Protocol demanded I see the operation before I agreed to do business with them.

I pulled into a small gravel lot and parked outside a ramshackle structure with a sign above the door proclaiming I'd arrived at "Miguel's Pizza." If it wasn't for Martin waiting for me outside the door, I'd have pulled out, sure I'd made a mistake. Martin took me inside the tiny wooden building and gave me a tour of the shop that was nested inside Miguel's, and we discussed business. None of that took very long. It was obvious that Search for Adventure would never be a very lucrative enterprise, but the shop already had a decent array of legitimate climbing brands on the shelves, comprising a nicely merchandised selection of hardware and simple climbing garb. The only missing headliner was Chouinard Equipment. I agreed to open an account for him.

Martin was amped to give me a tour of the climbing, so we hopped into his pickup truck, a monster vehicle with enough ground clearance to smoothly pass over small sports cars without a bump. We drove onto deeply rutted dirt paths in the thick green forest that coated the Red's rolling hills and gulches, passing occasional oil derricks and storage tanks. As Martin navigated the rough forest tracks, I couldn't see a cliff anywhere, and it was only after we'd parked and walked up a short hill that I finally spotted stone through the dense foliage. Martin had me lead a couple of moderate crack routes that I didn't find particularly memorable, but he was impressed enough by my climbing to drive me farther into the woods to explore more cliffs.

Martin was a big guy, a muscular mesomorph, and, as I learned from our short acquaintance, a strictly traditional climber. I asked him if he ever thought about bolting up some of the steep, highly featured faces I saw as we toured around. There was obviously huge potential. Even though sport climbing was now an accepted practice at many areas, Martin made it clear he didn't give a shit about sport climbing, quoting a common trope used by some traditional diehards: "Sport climbing is neither." He said he and his friends saw no need for bolting up faces since there were enough cracks to climb in the Red to keep anyone busy for a lifetime. Though I disagreed with him, I took a quick liking to Martin as we tooled around those red cliffs. But the more rock I saw, the crazier it seemed that he wouldn't even think of the potential for sport climbing. Arguing wasn't going to change his mind, and I saw no need to antagonize my newest Chouinard Equipment dealer, so I kept my mouth shut.

Later in the afternoon, back at Miguel's, I met the eponymous man himself. Miguel was slender and tall, with olive skin and dark hair with a few wisps of gray. He was busily shuffling around the room in a distracted fashion. Aside from the climbing gear and a few accessories, the only other money-maker at Miguel's was an ice-cream freezer filled with pints of Haagen-Dazs, sometimes purchased by state-park visitors on their way out of the gorge. When I inquired about a pizza, since his signage advertised that he sold them, Miguel gave me a puzzled look.

"Mercy, I have to see what we have," he said.

He poked around the shelves in his pantry. "Let's see, I have some spiral pasta and some black beans."

In a feat I thought rather impressive, Miguel produced an edible pizza with, yes, black beans and spiral pasta. Even as Miguel had worked his culinary magic, I did not think his restaurant-cum-climbing-shop had a very bright future.

On the drive back to Lexington, I stopped to use the pay phone at a rest area beside the main highway, calling the Chouinard office back in Ventura to check for messages. The receptionist had no messages for me, but said Peter needed to talk to me for a moment. That was nothing unusual. Metcalf and I often had talks about what was going on in the field while I was on the road.

Peter got right to the big news: "Russ, we got chaptered today."

"What?!" I said.

Metcalf explained that legal counsel had advised Yvon to divest himself of Chouinard Equipment, and just that morning, the employees of Chouinard Equipment had started their work week by being informed their company was filing for Chapter 11 protection under bankruptcy laws. There were four lawsuits pending against the company, all because of the plaintiffs misusing gear and all of the instances, save one, involving non-climbers. (If you purchase climbing gear today, you will note it comes with extensive warning language and instructions. The demise of Chouinard Equipment was the start of that trend—up to that time, the industry assumed buyers knew what they were doing.) The fear was potential financial damage to Patagonia, since both Chouinard Equipment and Patagonia were under the same corporate umbrella, the Lost Arrow Corporation. If a plaintiff's lawyer broke the shield separating Chouinard Equipment as a separate entity, Patagonia's assets could be at risk. Chouinard was a tiny business then, around six million dollars a year in total sales. Patagonia, however, was way bigger and growing way more quickly.

After Peter explained what had gone down that day in distant Ventura, my next question was, "Well, am I now on vacation, or do I still have a job?" Metcalf confirmed I still had payroll coming my way, but we also had some serious issues to address.

Even in that pre-social-media world, we knew news would travel fast. I was going to be on the road for several more weeks before returning to California, and my new task was to assure dealers that Chouinard Equipment was still in business and shipping gear.

When I got back to Ventura, the office mood was somber. With only sixty or so employees, Chouinard was as much a family as a workplace. A few folks had already given their notice, and more people trickled out the door over the next few weeks. When the leakage finally stopped, about a third of our workforce had split. At first, the hope was someone would buy us. After all, we were a leading company in the climbing-gear world—who wouldn't be interested?

As it turned out, in the down economy and tight monetary situation of 1989, no one was coming to our Chapter 11 door holding a bouquet of roses. Seeking a solution, Metcalf figured out that the only potential buyers were us, the employees. With pitbull determination and infectious optimism, he and Maria Cranor led the charge on the buyout, with those of us still left at Chouinard adding new chores to our normal workloads while the company muddled through Chapter 11. With a ridiculous amount of effort, including all of us cajoling money from friends, family, and vendors—and putting our own savings on the line—the buyout came together. On December 1, 1989, the transition was complete and Black Diamond Equipment was created. Richard Leversee, a Sierra Nevada climbing legend and the only other sales rep besides myself who'd stuck around, recalled, "Those were some magical times, and, hell yes, these were clearly miracles of the highest order that we pulled off the buyout of Chouinard and the creation of BD. [It was] sheer badassery with a bit of ill-advised, reckless abandon thrown in! Wow, what a ride!"

Amen, brother.

Over the course of the next year, the company made plans to vacate Ventura, which was a great place to live for a surfer, but not ideal for either climbing or backcountry skiing, the activities Black Diamond created gear for. Salt Lake City, at the foot of the Wasatch Mountains, would become the company's home, but not

Russ on "Merlin's Wand," Wadi Rum, Jordan
Photo: Amy Pickering

my own—my heart still lay in the Gunks. I'd purchased some land
there while I was in grad school and was ready to move back and
build a house. Since I traveled so much for work, it didn't really
matter if I was in the home office anyway, and Metcalf agreed to
my plan. So, in early 1991, after four years in Ventura and three of
those living in a garage, I packed up and drove back East.

I settled into my new house, a small saltbox with a large back
field and a lovely view of Millbrook Mountain, one of the ridge's
most imposing walls, a few miles distant. Being back felt right;
I belonged here. I reveled in the ability to take a quick ride to
the crag for a lunchtime bouldering session or a few after-work
pitches. Going for runs around the carriage roads in the early
mornings, spooking deer as I trotted, and getting immersed in
the thick greenness of the place was rejuvenating. It took no time
to fall back into the swing of climbing those big overhangs and
grabbing a Gunks bucket or crimping a fingertip edge. In a way, it

was almost as if I'd never left, except for the changes in the crowd. Some of my old friends had moved away, but there was never any lack of partners. Climbing had boomed over those four years while I was gone.

In August 1992, I made one last appearance at the ISPO trade show in Munich. I would soon be handing over the reins for the export business to others at Black Diamond, and limit my job responsibilities to repping along the East Coast. As I always did with any trip to Germany, I'd carved out a few days to go to Oberschollenbach to visit with Wolfgang, Kurt, and Norbert, making plans with Wolfgang to meet at his house and go climb before the show began. Maria Cranor, as she often did, joined me on that trip. We landed in Munich early in the morning of August 29, got our rental car, and headed north to the Frankenjura, a two-hour blast up the autobahn.

We arrived to an empty home. I checked for the stashed house key—still in the same place it had always been—and we let ourselves inside. We were dead tired from the flight and lay on the living room floor, falling into a jet-lagged nap while we waited for Wolfgang. The phone rang, but I ignored it. A few minutes later it rang again, but I was too sleepy to bother getting up. When it rang a third time, I finally rose to answer. Norbert, in a quivering voice, told me that Wolfgang had been in a very bad car accident on the autobahn. He'd left the house early that morning to do a radio interview in Munich and was returning home to meet us. He'd apparently fallen asleep at the wheel and veered off the pavement into a tree. He'd been driving over one hundred miles per hour—not an unusual speed on the West German highways, but one that demands concentration.

My stomach dropped. I wasn't hearing this; I was still sleeping and this was just a nightmare. But I wasn't sleeping. I was standing there, phone to my ear in Wolfgang's home, listening to Norbert tell me that something terrible had happened. Maria and I must have passed the crash site scant hours after Wolfgang's accident, but we'd seen no evidence of it. Norbert said Wolfgang was in critical condition, but he didn't have any other details. All we could do was wait for more information. Maria and I didn't know what else to do, so we did what Wolfgang would have suggested: we went climbing and hoped to hear better news later. It was not to be.

Norbert returned from the hospital in the evening, his face drawn with a sadness that remains etched in my memory. Wolfgang was on life-support machines, with no brain activity. I didn't want to believe it; I couldn't believe it. I had a restless, sleepless night wondering if there was a chance Wolf would pull through. In the morning, we drank our coffee quietly, each of us lost in our thoughts. Eventually, Maria and I went climbing, as much to keep our minds off Wolfgang's condition as anything else, but the usual joy of crimping our way up Frankenjura limestone was dulled by Wolfgang's conspicuous absence. When we got back to the house later that night, the news was no better. Wolf was brain dead, relying on life-support machines to keep his body alive.

I went down to the basement, where I'd spent so many nights. I stared at the pile of sleeping bags, mats, and bivy sacks piled up in a corner, looking like they were ready to be packed at a moment's notice, or maybe just discarded forever. The old homemade hangboard was still nailed above the doorway, with remnant chalk rimming the holds. Posters, taped up years ago and unchanged, plastered the walls, speaking of an unquenchable desire to explore, to climb hard, to enjoy life. The musty cellar smell was familiar and comforted me some, but now it felt like an echo of another life, another time, when all I had to worry about was what to climb next. Back when I was a climber who sometimes worked rather than a worker drone who sometimes climbed. Back when Wolfgang was alive.

I reached for the light switch. Above it, written in Sharpie, was the same message that had greeted me during my first night in the basement eight years before: *Gute Nacht.*

On Monday, August 31, 1992, the doctors at the hospital in Ingolstadt switched off Wolfgang Güllich's life support and declared him dead.

As much as I loved climbing in the Frankenjura, and enjoyed my time with friends there, with Wolfgang gone it would never be the same. When I left the house on Moselstrasse to return to Munich for the trade show, it was the last time I ever visited the area. After the ISPO show, I used work as my excuse for not staying another week for Wolfgang's funeral: I had appointments in France on my calendar. But all that was bullshit—just a convenient justification. I've never been one for funerals, and funerals of great friends are even harder for me. I'd seen most everyone I wanted to commiserate with at the trade show, and I didn't want my last image of Wolfgang to be of his corpse or a grave marker. I needed him to remain in my mind as a smiling face, still very much alive, joking on my lack of progress on a project and suggesting it was time for a piece of cake and some coffee. Maybe that's selfish. Maybe it's just how I cope with good friends dying.

I'd been lucky enough to climb with a lot of great partners over the years, many of the best climbers of my generation. As with any group, some were more fun to be around than others.

Some were super serious about their climbing, while some were super good at climbing and happy to let you know it. But very few were like Wolfgang. The man who introduced 5.14a, 5.14b, and—in a thunderbolt—5.14d to the climbing lexicon wasn't just a powerhouse of ability. He was incredibly fun to be with.

I didn't always feel comfortable around celebrity climbers, those who were substantially better than me, and whom I sometimes found intimidating. My own insecurities could bubble up in pressure situations, be it an effort to climb a hard route or perform well under cliff-base scrutiny. I never felt that way with Wolfgang, even though his abilities far outstripped mine. He was so approachable, so utterly friendly. He could be having a shitty day at the crag and still laugh. He was always down for the midday break for coffee and cake. Wolfgang brought out the best in me when we climbed together. When I didn't believe in myself, he would pick up the slack, saying, "Come on, it's not so hard for you! You looked good last try!" We even shared a girlfriend. When I left Germany shortly after the Bardonecchia competition and our *Team Motivation* route, he and his neighbor Gabi started a relationship for a time. I couldn't have been happier. He was a brother.

I still miss him to this day.

EPILOGUE

In June 1988, the year after I started work at Chouinard Equipment, the first-ever professional climbing competition on US soil was held at The Cliff Lodge at the Snowbird ski resort in Utah, with the side of the lodge transformed into a huge climbing wall. Competition climbing had become all the rage in Europe, much as I'd figured it might, and the United States was playing catch-up. The wall was composed of manufactured panels slapped onto the side of the lodge, creating a 115-foot vertical "cliff" with a big wave of an overhang shortly before the slabby top. In order to make the routes difficult enough, the setters had to use tiny holds, which made the routes technical and painful on the fingers.

While I wouldn't be competing, I went out to Snowbird anyway, to spectate and see old friends. It felt weird at first, seeing my colleagues in their competition tank tops joking and bantering while warming up. Some asked why I wasn't partaking, especially in an American event. I looked at the wall and admitted that I was curious, but I knew that the pressure-cooker environment of competitions would never be for me, even as many of my friends reveled in it. I was content to cheer them on.

The men's finals played out as if scripted by Hollywood. Climber after talented climber came out and did their damndest to complete the pitch. Most didn't get halfway up, and nobody made it through the overhang. Then the number-one seed from the qualifying rounds, Patrick Edlinger—a French superstar nicknamed "Le Blond" and known for his grace on the rock—came out as the final competitor. He moved up the wall as if the holds were enormous. Every move looked smooth, elegant, and almost effortless. The crowd's shouts grew louder as Patrick passed the highest point anyone had yet reached. He kept going, and the crowd yelled louder. He attacked the overhang like he was tapping the energy pulsing from the spectators below, pulling the lip just as the sun broke through the clouds and lit his flowing mane. He'd smashed it.

Patrick lowered to the ground, radiant, knowing he'd just put on a hell of a show. He saw me in the crowd and called me over. I gave him a hug of congratulations, amazed at what he'd just done and recalling my debate with Wolfgang about the future of competition climbing all those years earlier. With the rousing success of Snowbird, as embodied by Patrick's performance, this new genre had caught fire. Today, climbing is an Olympic event, and with climbing teams and youth programs at virtually every gym in the world, competition climbing is as much a part of everyday life as Little League baseball and soccer.

With a somewhat reduced travel schedule, I finally had time to cook a meal in my own kitchen. That was a good thing, since I'd met the woman I'd marry as I moved into my new house in New Paltz in May of 1991.

Russ on "Life is a Fairytale," Tsaranoro, Madagascar, 2017

Diane worked part-time at an outdoor shop in Amherst, Massachusetts, while earning her MBA at UMass. We'd met while I did a gear clinic for the shop staff and had hit it off immediately. She started climbing with me and picked it up quickly. That wasn't a huge surprise, since she was a natural athlete and had been an Olympian for the 1988 US field-hockey team in Seoul, South Korea.

Most of my old reliable ropemates were gone. Jeff Gruenberg had moved to the South, where he continued to climb and put up new routes. Jack Mileski had been teaching school in Texas before moving to Colorado, and Mike Freeman was working for *Climbing* magazine, also in Colorado. Lynn Hill had moved to France, where she rose to a level of climbing far above what she'd accomplished while she lived in New Paltz. As I was moving back to the Gunks, she became the first woman to redpoint a 5.14.

While Scott Franklin had left, living part-time in France and part time in Bend, Oregon, his favorite partners, Al Diamond and Jordan Mills, were still living in New Paltz and climbing at a high standard. It wasn't long before I was climbing with them and other folks newer to the scene. At thirty-two years of age, I was perhaps now the "old man" in the group, but that didn't matter to me or to my partners in our shared passion. Through the 1990s and into the early 2000s, we did a stack of new, hard routes in the Gunks, but often as topropes—there was too little in the way of protection for my appetite. I was now too old to die young, and didn't embrace getting the shit scared out of me anymore.

One tragic loss to the Gunks scene during my absence was that of Kevin Bein, the "Mayor of the Gunks." Kevin had climbed in the Gunks since the 1960s, often with his wife, Barbara Devine. Strong as a bull, with a perpetual smile and positive attitude, Kevin was a "best friend" to just about everyone who knew him; he was an endlessly patient and supportive belayer, and just the person you wanted with you when trying a hard route. In the summer of 1988, he and Barbara took a trip to Europe to do some alpine climbing as a change from their usual diet of cragging. On the Matterhorn, they turned back from their ascent in the face of deteriorating weather. A rappel anchor gave way. Fortunately for Barbara, she was not clipped into it, but she was left stranded and having to be rescued after watching her husband fall out of sight to his death. I heard that at Kevin's memorial service, Steve Wunsch, the first ascensionist of *Supercrack*, said that Kevin's positive energy was responsible for getting most of his partners up their hardest routes. Steve counted himself as one of those.

One morning I got a phone call from Gruenberg. I'd see Jeff on occasion when I was down south climbing or working in the Chattanooga, Tennessee, area, but since we didn't keep in constant contact, the phone call was unusual. I heard bad news in his voice immediately. He told me, as he choked back sobs, that Jack Mileski had been shot to death by an estranged girlfriend. The man who'd introduced the phrase "beta" to the climbing lexicon was gone.

In October of 1999, I was in the Red River Gorge, climbing with my pal Jonny Woodward and sharing a campfire with a group of Patagonia employees, when word of Alex Lowe's death in an avalanche on Shishapangma, an 8,000-meter peak in China, stilled the evening laughter. Another icon of American climbing lost. Seven years later, another shock came when Todd Skinner died when his harness belay loop failed while he was rappelling in Yosemite Valley. In 2010, Kurt Albert, the man who'd invented the redpoint concept, died in a via ferrata accident in Bavaria. Kurt's death left Norbert Sandner as the only remaining survivor

Hayden Kennedy, Amy Pickering, Lynn Hill, Jonny Woodward (LtR) at a climbers party in Salt Lake City

of the original gang at the house on Moselstrasse. My generation, my old partners, were disappearing like leaves off an autumn tree. I think of these old partners, my friends, frequently and I feel the drumbeat reminder that it's always later than you think.

My bet on Miguel's Pizza in the Red River Gorge, after my initial visit to the area in 1989, could not have been more off base. I didn't think Miguel or his pizza joint had a chance in hell of making it. How wrong I was. Once the drilling started in the early 1990s and expansion bolts were placed, sport climbing in the Red exploded in popularity. Conflict with the diehard traditionalists was short lived, with the sport climbers outnumbering them and overwhelmingly making their case. Word spread quickly around the country and Miguel's parking lot became a crowded hub of vans and pickups full of climbers ready to test their endurance on the steep, pocketed walls. The Red even caught fire with the Europeans, something rarely seen in the United States. With all those great crags everywhere across the Atlantic, why bother travelling to America? Turns out, for the Red River Gorge. During the peak, autumn climbing season, Miguel's now sounds like the United Nations, with Spanish, German, French, and Italian being spoken in the backwoods of Kentucky. With tens of thousands of climbers coming through, Miguel has expanded his operation to such a degree that the business became one of the largest employers in Powell County, bringing jobs to one of the poorest counties in the country. The large fields behind the main buildings, once the habitat for his small goat herd, transformed into a campground reserved for climbers only, teeming with a sea of Sprinter vans and tents. The original gear shop, Search for Adventure, didn't make the cut and Martin Hackworth moved out of the area, but in its place is, of course, Miguel's own climbing shop, which cranks. The family business has boomed.

I continued my work, repping for Black Diamond, for another twenty-five years after moving back to the Gunks. The lifestyle suited me, with daily flexibility to schedule climbing while back home, and more trips to other crags while on the road. An unfortunate side effect of the chronic, nomadic lifestyle was the strain on my marriage. Being away from home for weeks at a time put a distance between Diane and me that eventually became too large to bridge. When we had our daughter, Mayv, the cracks in our relationship turned into chasms. We were both strong personalities and didn't give in to the other's desires easily. In the end, after eight years married, we split up. Once we did, and got over the initial anger and disappointment, we became better friends than ever, certainly a benefit to our lovely daughter. Mayv showed promise in climbing, being able to latch holds and climb out overhanging walls in my home gym at two years old, but in the end, she followed mom's footsteps and became an elite field-hockey player. I was good with that. She found a passion to help direct her life, and I don't think any parent can ask for more.

One week, while I was away for work, my partner, Amy Pickering, sorted through a bunch of old print photos I had in a box in my office. The pictures were just a random selection of crap snapshots I'd collected over the years. Amy framed a bunch of those photos and hung them along a couple walls in our house. They are reminders of friends I still see and some I'll never see again. Mileski is up there, along with Wolfgang. A grinning Kurt Albert dangles from a cliff dressed in lederhosen and hanging from one hand, while the other hand grasps a gigantic stein of beer. Skinner grins in a group shot from the speed-climbing trip, while Lowe dangles from a Millbrook overhang. Kevin Bein stands at the base of *Supercrack* with Lynn and other friends, and Jerry Moffatt is mugging at the Bardonecchia competition.

I look at these pictures often and I am reminded how lucky I have been to be a climber, and how climbing is not so much about the routes we climb but instead about the kinships and love created by sharing a rope with friends. I remain in awe at where climbing has brought me. Life is serendipitous, indeed. It's not just all the amazing places and cliffs around the world I got to see, but it's also the career I ended up in, one that allowed me the freedom to climb and still pay the bills. If I'd not met Maria Cranor, Peter Metcalf never would have offered me a job, and if Yvon Chouinard had not declared Chapter 11 bankruptcy, there would have been no Black Diamond. Heaven forbid, I might have ended up a lawyer.

Despite the loss of dear friends and an ever-creakier body, climbing has never lost its appeal. Neither has the desire to seek out new places. I still travel frequently to explore new countries and new climbing areas and make new acquaintances. The differences between my travels in the 1980s and now is so stark. Information on anything and everything and everyone is just one click away, but forty years ago we climbers could only find the rock, and each other, through letter writing, pay phones, and magazine articles. Certainly, the crags are a lot more crowded now. In the heart of my full-time climbing career, I could expect to see a familiar face at almost any cliff I visited, anywhere in the world—our tribe of rock climbers was that small. Now, I can't expect to go to a climbing area and see familiar faces unless I've arranged it, despite the wave of humanity I find there.

The Gunks remain home, though after almost five decades of grabbing its holds and contorting my way out its overhangs, I've pretty much squeezed all the adventure I can from these cliffs. And as each year passes, it seems the holds get smaller while

Russ and his daughter, Mayv, on Kilimanjaro, 2022

the overhangs just get bigger. When I gaze up at Millbrook over morning coffee, I'm flooded with memories and reminded how much these cliffs can teach us about ourselves. I feel more and more like a partner in a long-term, mature relationship with my beloved Gunks as they teach me, again and again, that it ain't all about the grade I'm climbing. It's about the memories, and what we learn about ourselves while we're making them.

AUTHOR BIO

Photo: Andy Earl

Russ Clune is a rock climber living in the Shawangunk Mountains of New York. His articles have been published in multiple journals, including *Climbing, Rock & Ice, Mountain, Alpinist, Der Bergsteiger, Iwa To Yuki, The Patagonia Catalog,* and *Urban Climber.* Clune has been climbing for over forty-five years and was one of America's best rock climbers during his peak in the 1980s. He is also one of the world's most well-traveled rock climbers. Clune was part of the employee group that created the leading climbing-gear company, Black Diamond Equipment, where he worked for thirty years. He remains an active climber and continues to travel the globe seeking new adventures.

ACKNOWLEDGEMENTS

This book wouldn't have happened without the help of a lot of folks. First off, I'm grateful I got to work with the people at Di Angelo Publications. Sequoia Schmidt and her team helped shepherd my work to the finished product, including hooking me up with Matt Samet as my editor. Matt's skillful editing and extensive climbing knowledge was fundamental to getting my book honed, and it was pure pleasure working with such a talented author and editor.

The Lifer went through a ton of iterations—even before getting to final editing—and many people had a hand in helping me out in that process. I am indebted to Susan Fox Rogers, whose advice and chops as a writer, editor, and English professor helped me through my first several versions. William Finnegan's Pulitzer Prize winning memoir about his surfing life, *Barbarian Days*, served as motivation for me to start my own project. Bill became a friend and mentor, and his advice was gold; a 5.15 writer giving a 5.8 upstart tips on how to get off the ground. Amy Pickering painstakingly read several drafts and questioned the relevance of certain passages to the greater theme, helping me focus on what I really wanted to say, and Kenneth Wapner helped guide me to structuring the manuscript into a digestible format.

Others who read early segments or drafts and whose comments helped me include Sam Elias, Andy Salo, Arthur Sulzberger, Pete Takeda, Jeff Smoot, Ken Wohlrob, and Tara Clune. Relying on journals and photos got me far, but I also needed to check my memory with those involved with various episodes, and for that, I owe thanks to Melinda Rutledge Hood, Lynn Hill, Alan Watts, Roger "Strappo" Hughes, Jim Gilchrist, Jerry Moffatt, Pete O'Donovan, and Peter Metcalf.

A big thanks to Beth Wald, Andy Earl, and Matt Calardo for use of their photographs, and to my brothers, Kevin and Tim, who questioned the wisdom of including details of our childhood antics.

Lastly and perhaps most importantly, a heartfelt thanks to all I had the privilege to share a rope with over the decades!